BBC MUSIC

STRAUSS TON

D. RENSHAW

BBC MUSIC GUIDES

Bach Cantatas J. A. WESTRUP
Bach Organ Music PETER WILLIAMS
Bartók Chamber Music STEPHEN WALSH
Bartók Orchestral Music JOHN MCCABE
Beethoven Concertos and Overtures ROGER FISKE
Beethoven Piano Sonatas DENIS MATTHEWS
Beethoven String Quartets BASIL LAM
Beethoven Symphonies ROBERT SIMPSON
Berlioz Orchestral Music HUGH MACDONALD
Brahms Chamber Music IVOR KEYS
Brahms Orchestral Music JOHN MORTON
Brahms Piano Music DENIS MATTHEWS
Brahms Songs ERIC SAMS
Bruckner Symphonies PHILIP BARFORD
Couperin DAVID TUNLEY
Debussy Orchestral Music DAVID COX
Debussy Piano Music FRANK DAWES
Dvořák Symphonies and Concertos ROBERT LAYTON
Elgar Orchestral Music MICHAEL KENNEDY
Falla RONALD CRICHTON
Gesualdo DENIS ARNOLD
Handel Concertos STANLEY SADIE
Haydn String Quartets ROSEMARY HUGHES
Haydn Symphonies H. C. ROBBINS LANDON
Hugo Wolf Songs MOSCO CARNER
Mahler Symphonies and Songs PHILIP BARFORD
Mendelssohn Chamber Music JOHN HORTON
Monteverdi Church Music DENIS ARNOLD
Monteverdi Madrigals DENIS ARNOLD
Mozart Chamber Music A. HYATT KING
Mozart Piano Concertos PHILIP RADCLIFFE
Mozart Serenades, Divertimenti and Dances ERIK SMITH
Mozart Wind and String Concertos A. HYATT KING
Purcell ARTHUR HUTCHINGS
Rachmaninov Orchestral Music PATRICK PIGGOTT
Ravel Orchestral Music LAURENCE DAVIES
Schoenberg Chamber Music ARNOLD WHITTALL
Schubert Chamber Music J. A. WESTRUP
Schubert Piano Sonatas PHILIP RADCLIFFE
Schubert Songs MAURICE J. E. BROWN
Schubert Symphonies MAURICE J. E. BROWN
Schumann Orchestral Music HANS GAL
Schumann Piano Music JOAN CHISSELL
Schumann Songs ASTRA DESMOND
Shostakovich Symphonies HUGH OTTAWAY
Szymanowski CHRISTOPHER PALMER
Tchaikovsky Ballet Music JOHN WARRACK
Tchaikovsky Symphonies and Concertos JOHN WARRACK
The Trio Sonata CHRISTOPHER HOGWOOD
Vaughan Williams Symphonies HUGH OTTAWAY
Vivaldi MICHAEL TALBOT

BBC MUSIC GUIDES

Strauss Tone Poems

MICHAEL KENNEDY

BRITISH BROADCASTING CORPORATION

The music examples are reproduced by kind permission of the following: Exx. 1–22, copyright 1932 assigned to C. F. Peters Musikverlag, Peters Editions Ltd, London, reprinted by permission of the publishers. Exx. 23–5, 29, 32, copyright F. E. C. Leuckart Musikverlag, Munich, reprinted by permission of Fentone Music Ltd. Exx. 26–8, copyright © 1904 Bote & Bock, Berlin, printed by kind permission of G. Schirmer Ltd, London. Ex. 33 reprinted by kind permission of Boosey & Hawkes Music Publishers Ltd.

Quotations from Mary Whittall's translation of *Richard Strauss: a Chronicle of the Early Years 1864–1898* by Willi Schuh are printed by kind permission of Cambridge University Press.

Published by the
British Broadcasting Corporation
35 Marylebone High Street
London W1M 4AA

ISBN 0 563 20275 0

First published 1984

© Michael Kennedy 1984

Filmset in Great Britain by
August Filmsetting, Haydock, St. Helens.
Printed in England by Hollen Street Press, Slough, Berks

Contents

The Era of the Tone Poem	7
Macbeth	13
Don Juan	17
Tod und Verklärung	21
Till Eulenspiegel	25
Also sprach Zarathustra	29
Don Quixote	34
Ein Heldenleben	40
Symphonia Domestica	48
Eine Alpensinfonie	54
Aftermath	61
Strauss's Recordings	68
List of Works Discussed	68

To Bernard Benoliel

The Era of the Tone Poem

If we exclude the early 'symphonic fantasy' *Aus Italien* and the two large-scale orchestral works with 'symphony' in their title (*Domestic* and *Alpine*), Richard Strauss wrote seven tone poems between 1886 and 1898 (between the age of twenty-two and thirty-four). Six of these are in the regular repertoire of the world's leading symphony orchestras. The brilliance of their scoring, the memorability of their melodies and the immediacy of their impact commend them to audiences, performers and conductors alike. No series of orchestral concerts is complete without one or several of them. When they were new, they outraged conventional opinion. Today, when they are generally regarded as romantic classics, they still arouse controversy between those who rank Strauss as a great composer and those who find him flawed by spiritual and aesthetic deficiencies, a cynical manipulator of listeners (most of whom are only too willing and happy to be manipulated by such a master). While *Don Juan* and *Till Eulenspiegel* are admitted even by Straussophobes to be works of genius, there is less unanimity over *Tod und Verklärung, Also sprach Zarathustra* and *Ein Heldenleben*: echoes of shibboleths still cling to them. For this survey – of the shibboleths as well as of the tone poems – I have begun with *Aus Italien* and have included the *Domestic* and *Alpine* symphonies, which are tone poems before they are symphonies. (Tone poem (*Tondichtung*) was the term Strauss himself coined and which he preferred to symphonic poem.)

The heyday of the symphonic poem lasted about seventy years, from 1850 to 1920. Briefly, the symphonic poem is the most concentrated manifestation of programme music, i.e. music which tells a story or is deliberately descriptive. (All music, of course, is to some extent programmatic.) Music's onomatopoeic characteristics are no nineteenth-century discovery: they have existed for as long as music itself. Battle scenes occur in the earliest music, so do storms and birdsong. Vivaldi's *The Four Seasons* is a string of tone poems. Yet the form may be ascribed principally to the nineteenth century. There are symphonic poems for a solo instrument such as the piano, and for a chamber group, but use of a symphony orchestra is implied by the term. The symphonic poem chimed in perfectly with the Romantic's wish for interrelationship of all the arts and especially the interaction of music and literature. Thus the drama of the opera house was imported into the concert hall. In addition, the invention, development and improvement of instruments, and the consequent enlargement of the symphony orchestra, with the widening and intensifying of its expressive capabilities, encouraged composers to attain a more sophisticated and complex style. Not only could the sounds of nature be imitated in music, but the characters of men and women, their ideals and emotions, could be described. The two works which advanced the range of programme music were Beethoven's 'Pastoral' Symphony (1808) and Berlioz's *Symphonie fantastique* (1831), but the true ancestors of the Straussian tone poem were the more concise, one-movement works officially designated 'overtures' – Beethoven's *Egmont* (1809), *Coriolan* (1807) and *Leonore No. 3* (1806), Mendelssohn's *Hebrides* (1830) and *A Midsummer Night's Dream* (1826). Schumann's concert overtures were in this line, emulated half a century later by Elgar in *Froissart* (1890), *Cockaigne* (1901) and *In the South* (1904). The chief developer of the genre, however, was Liszt, who composed two programme symphonies, the *Faust* and the *Dante*, and a series of twelve one-movement symphonic poems (his own term) while he was at Weimar between 1848 and 1861. Liszt's symphonic poems, which include *Les Préludes* (1848), *Mazeppa* (1851), *Die Ideale* (1857) and *Orpheus* (1854), are less descriptive than Strauss's; his use of the epithet 'symphonic' is the clue to his aim to give a binding inner symphonic logic and thematic development to his single-movement structures, however loosely episodic their outward form. In his orchestration of the earlier symphonic poems Liszt was assisted by Raff, who went on to compose eleven symphonies on nature subjects (No. 7, of 1875, is *In the Alps*).

Liszt's example was followed more enthusiastically in Bohemia, Russia and France than in Germany. Smetana, after visiting Weimar in 1857, composed symphonic poems on literary subjects, including *Richard III* (1858, Shakespeare) and *Wallenstein's Camp* (1859, Schiller), but his finest achievement is the cycle of six called *Má Vlast* (*My Country*) (1874–9). His fellow-countrymen Dvořák, Fibich, Janáček, Novák, Foerster and Suk all wrote impressive examples. In Russia Balakirev's *Tamara* (1867–82), Borodin's *In the Steppes of Central Asia* (1880) and Glazunov's *Stenka Razin* (1885) are outclassed by Tchaikovsky's *Romeo and Juliet* (1869, rev. 1880), *Francesca da Rimini* (1876) and *Hamlet* (1888), all masterly musical treatments of a literary subject, as is his large-scale programmatic symphony based on Byron's *Manfred* (1885). In France the leading purveyors of symphonic poems were Saint-Saëns, with *Le rouet d'Omphale* (1871), *Danse macabre* (1874) and *La jeunesse d'Hercule* (1877); D'Indy, with the *Wallenstein* trilogy (1874–82); Duparc, with *Lénore* (1875); Franck, with *Les Éolides* (1876) and *Le chasseur maudit* (1882); and Dukas, with his brilliant Goethe scherzo *L'apprenti-sorcier* (1897). There is no narrative, merely exquisite evocation of emotion and sensuality, in Debussy's *L'après-midi d'un faune* (1892–4), but it is a symphonic poem nevertheless. Indeed, few are more symphonic and more poetic. The exotically orchestrated genre of tone poem reached its final gaudy brilliance in Italy in the 1920s in the works of Respighi (*The Fountains of Rome, The Pines of Rome, The Birds, Three Botticelli Pictures*). Messiaen's *Turangalîla* Symphony (1946–8) is a massive symphonic poem containing a Respighi-like sensuality of sound.

British composers turned to the form, it is reliably estimated, in 1892 when Wallace wrote *The Passing of Beatrice*. Elgar's overtures have already been mentioned but his major essay in the form was his 'symphonic study' *Falstaff* (1913). Harty (*With the Wild Geese* and *The Children of Lir*), Bax (*Tintagel, November Woods* and *The Garden of Fand*), Vaughan Williams (*In the Fen Country*), Delius (*Paris*), Bantock (*Fifine at the Fair*) and Bridge (*Summer*) all found an outlet for their considerable descriptive powers in symphonic poems, perhaps in some cases stimulated by the series written by Sibelius, whose music was admired in Britain as much as it was in his native Finland. The composers who came to maturity in Britain after 1920 – Walton, Britten and Tippett chief among them – found the form outdated, although Britten's *Sea Interludes* from his opera *Peter Grimes* are effectively symphonic poems of the highest distinction, as are the *Ritual Dances* from Tippett's *The Midsummer Marriage*. Lately Harrison Birtwistle, Jonathan Harvey and Robin Holloway have composed symphonic poems.

In Germany only a handful of composers trod this Lisztian path and it did not include the giants Wagner and Brahms, nor Bruckner and Mahler. In 1885 Hugo Wolf completed his *Penthesilea*; from Schoenberg in 1899 there came *Verklärte Nacht* (programmatic chamber music) and *Pelleas und Melisande* in 1902–3. The minor figure Alexander Ritter (1833–96), who married Wagner's niece and worked with Liszt, wrote several Lisztian tone poems. An orchestral violinist, it was while he was at Meiningen playing under his friend Hans von Bülow that he met the 21-year-old Richard Strauss who, in 1885, had been invited by Bülow to be his assistant conductor.

Strauss was brought up in a strictly classical tradition. His early works are in line of descent from Schumann and Mendelssohn. His father, principal horn-player in the Munich Court Orchestra for forty-two years from 1847 to 1889, detested Wagner as man and musician and hoped his son would do likewise. When Strauss went to Meiningen he was in the full flush of Brahms-worship. But Ritter changed all that. He urged Strauss to follow Berlioz, Liszt and Wagner in developing the expressive element in music. In evenings at Ritter's home in Meiningen, and later in Munich, Strauss 'found an intellectual and spiritual stimulus which had a decisive effect on my future development'. He was introduced to Wagner's writings and to the philosophy of Schopenhauer. To quote Strauss again: 'New ideas must seek out new forms for themselves: the basic principle adopted by Liszt in his symphonic works, in which the poetic idea really did act simultaneously as the structural element, became from then onwards the guideline for my own symphonic works.'[1]

Strauss made his way gingerly towards the Lisztian symphonic poem. In April and May 1886 he visited Italy for the first time where he was as impressed by the natural beauty – something to which he was always intensely responsive – as by the buildings and by works of art in the galleries. On his return to Munich he settled down to completion of a 'symphonic fantasy' he had sketched during his holiday. This was *Aus Italien*, Op. 16, completed on 12 September 1886 and dedicated to Bülow. The first performance was conducted by Strauss in Munich on 2 March 1887 (with his father playing first horn after 'practising the difficult, audacious solos . . . at home long before the day'[2]). The work had a mixed reception which Strauss, as he wrote to a woman friend, 'found tremendous fun. . . Some of them applauded furiously, some of them hissed vigorously, in the end the applause won. The opposition have pronounced me half-crazy . . . I felt immensely proud: the first work to have met with the opposition of the multitude; that proves it must be of some significance.'

Today it seems incredible that this colourful, picturesque and melodious music could ever have been regarded as 'revolutionary'.

---

[1] Richard Strauss, 'Recollections of My Youth and Years of Apprenticeship' in *Recollections and Reflections* (Zürich, 1949).

[2] Johanna von Rauchenberger-Strauss (Strauss's sister), 'Youthful Memories' in *Richard Strauss Yearbook 1959–60*.

Bülow thought its composer was a genius but told Ritter that he thought the music went 'to the utmost limit of what is musically possible (within the bounds of beauty)'. Munich was upset by the fourth and last movement – in which Strauss quoted what he believed was a Neapolitan folksong, 'Funiculì, funiculà', and later discovered had been composed in 1880 by Luigi Denza – but when the Berlin Philharmonic played it in 1888 they 'burst out laughing, people have a sense of humour here' (Strauss's letter to his father after the concert). In his old age Strauss called *Aus Italien* 'a timid experiment' in his Lisztian conversion, but in a letter to a friend in 1887 he expressed views on the descriptive element in music from which he never demurred. Complaining that some writers had misunderstood the piece, he continued:

It consists of *sensations evoked by* the sight of the wonderful natural beauties of Rome and Naples, *not descriptions* of them . . . It really is ridiculous to suggest that a present-day composer, whose tutors have been the classics, especially late Beethoven, as well as Wagner and Liszt, would write a work three-quarters of an hour in length to show off with the kind of piquant tone-painting and brilliant instrumentation that almost every advanced composition student still at a conservatory can write nowadays. *Expression* is our art, and a piece of music which has nothing truly poetic to convey to me – content, that is, of course, which can be properly represented *only in music*, a content that words may be able to *suggest but only suggest* – a piece like that in my view is anything you care to call it, but not music.

Strauss's own description, written in 1889, of the four movements of *Aus Italien* is still worth quotation:

1. *On the Campagna: Andante* (G major). This prelude, which reproduces the mood experienced by the composer at the sight of the broad extent of the Roman Campagna bathed in sunlight, as seen from the Villa d'Este at Tivoli, is based on three principal themes . . .

2. *In the Ruins of Rome: Allegro con brio* (C major). Fantastic images of vanished glory, feelings of melancholy and grief amid the brilliant sunshine of the present . . . The formal structure of the movement is that of a big symphonic first movement.

3. *On the beach of Sorrento: Andantino* (A major). This movement essays the representation in tone-painting of the tender music of nature, which the inner ear hears in the rustling of the wind in the leaves, in birdsong and in all the delicate voices of nature, in the distant murmur of the sea, whence a solitary song reaches to the beach; and the contrasting of it with the sensations experienced by the human listener, which are expressed in the melodic elements of the movement.

4. *Neapolitan Folk-life: Allegro molto* . . . This crazy orchestral fantasy . . . attempts to depict the colourful bustle of Naples in a hilarious jumble of themes.

The reasons *Aus Italien* is not played more frequently are its length and its unevenness. Elgar's *In the South* (1904), which covers similar ground, is a shorter, equally brilliant and wholly mature musical portrait of Italy. The best of *Aus Italien* is to be found in the Prelude; its three main themes are Straussian and anticipate melodies made familiar in the later tone poems. The sureness of the orchestration, while remarkable, will surprise no one who has heard the Symphony in D minor which Strauss wrote while still at school in 1880. Imitative of classical models though it may be, it has a fragrant charm because of the freshness and lucidity of its scoring. The 'Ruins of Rome' movement of *Aus Italien* has none of the grandeur of Elgar's evocation of 'the ancient day'. Although the development section and coda show Strauss in easy command of the structural element, the invention is less interesting. The rhythmic cut of the themes is Schumannesque, the woodwind writing pays homage to Brahms. There is more sense of individuality in the 'Sorrento' *Andantino*. The nature sounds have their origins in Siegfried's forest and there are foreshadowings of the waterfalls of the *Alpine Symphony* of nearly thirty years later in the cascades for flutes and violins. Strauss comes nearest to his Lisztian model in this movement, replacing the sonata-form development with a new and poetic episode. The light-hearted finale has been unjustly castigated. If Strauss mistook Denza's tune for a folksong, so what? His treatment of it is witty enough not to have needed to be dignified by his somewhat mechanical use of 'cyclic' form in briefly recalling themes from earlier movements.

This 'first step on the road towards independence', as Strauss described *Aus Italien* to Bülow, was followed almost immediately by his first one-movement symphonic poem, *Macbeth*, based on Shakespeare's play. *Aus Italien* he correctly saw as the bridge to this 'completely new path'. Before we follow Strauss up that new path, this seems the moment for a detailed list of his tone poems (whether or not they are so described on their title-page):

Macbeth, Op.23, tone poem (after Shakespeare). First version (unpublished) 1886–8; second version 1889–91. First performance (revised version): Weimar, 13 October 1890, Weimar Court Orchestra, conducted by Strauss; first performance of rescored revised version: Berlin, 29 February 1892, Berlin Philharmonic Orchestra, conducted by Strauss.

Don Juan, Op.20, tone poem, 1888. First performance: Weimar, 11 November 1889, Weimar Court Orchestra, conducted by Strauss.

Tod und Verklärung (Death and Transfiguration), Op.24, tone poem, 1888–9. First performance: Eisenach, 21 June 1890 (meeting of Allgemeiner Deutscher Musikverein), Eisenach Tonkünstlerfest, conducted by Strauss.

Till Eulenspiegels lustige Streiche, nach alter Schelmenweise in Rondeauform für grosses Orchester gesetzt (Till Eulenspiegel's merry pranks, after an old rogue's tale, set in rondo form for large orchestra), Op. 28, 1894–5. First performance: Cologne, Gürzenich concert,

5 November 1895, Cologne Gürzenich City Orchestra, conducted by Franz Wüllner.

Also sprach Zarathustra (Thus spake Zarathustra), Op.30, tone poem freely after Nietzsche, 1894–6. First performance: Frankfurt, 27 November 1896, Frankfurt Museum City Orchestra, conducted by Strauss.

Don Quixote, introduzione, tema con variazioni, finale. Fantastische Variationen über ein Thema ritterlichen Charakters (Fantastic Variations on a theme of Knightly Character), Op.35, 1896–7. First performance: Cologne Gürzenich concert, 8 March 1898, Cologne Gürzenich City Orchestra, conducted by Franz Wüllner (solo cellist Friedrich Grützmacher).

Ein Heldenleben (A Hero's Life), Op. 40, tone poem, 1897–8. First performance: Frankfurt, 3 March 1899, Frankfurt Museum City Orchestra, conducted by Strauss.

Symphonia Domestica (Domestic Symphony), Op. 53, 1902–3. First performance: New York (Carnegie Hall), 21 March 1904, Wetzler Orchestra, conducted by Strauss.

Eine Alpensinfonie (An Alpine Symphony), Op.64, 1911–15. First performance: Berlin, 28 October 1915, Dresden Court Orchestra, conducted by Strauss.

Macbeth, Op. 23

In spite of its opus number, *Macbeth* is the first of Strauss's tone poems, although it had its first performance after both *Don Juan* and *Tod und Verklärung*. This was because the work was put aside after completion and later revised. Strauss probably began to sketch it in the spring of 1887. It was completed early in 1888 and sent to Bülow, who criticised the ending (a triumphal march for Macduff), saying: 'It is quite in order for an *Egmont* overture to end with a march celebrating the triumph of Egmont, but a symphonic poem called *Macbeth* cannot end with the triumph of Macduff.' Strauss took the point. He was by now at work on *Don Juan*. He wrote to Bülow on 24 August 1888: 'For the time being *Macbeth* lies contentedly buried in my desk, while the dissonances will see if they can eat each other up. *Don Juan* will perhaps go to keep him company soon.' In this long letter he further explained his musical outlook to his mentor:

I still think it's better to follow one's true artistic conviction and to have said something wrong up a blind alley than something superfluous while keeping to the old, well-trodden high road . . . From my F minor Symphony onwards I have found myself trapped in a steadily growing antithesis between the musical-cum-poetic content that I have wanted to communicate and the form of the ternary sonata-movement which we have inherited from the classics . . . The precise expression of my artistic ideas and feelings and stylistically the most self-reliant of all my works to date, the one in which I was most conscious of my intentions, is *Macbeth*.

Strauss provided *Macbeth* with a new ending in 1889. It was almost certainly this revised version which he ran through with the Mannheim orchestra that year. But no public performance was given until 1890, at Weimar. Strauss was still dissatisfied, not with the structure but with the scoring. For five months, until 4 March 1891, he reworked the instrumentation. The second performance – in effect the first of the work as we know it today – was in Berlin on 29 February 1892, when the piece had a tremendous reception. Bülow, now converted to the work's worth, described its sound as 'overwhelming. The composer has never had a reception like this in Berlin before.' Strauss himself thought it 'fabulous . . . there's no longer a single theme that doesn't "stand out".'

Strauss cast *Macbeth* in sonata form, but in his own adaptation of it for his poetic purposes. The development section is much longer than the recapitulation and contains two independent episodes, each with a new theme. There is no attempt to follow the plot of Shakespeare's play in any detail – we are spared any Berlioz-like witches. As in Tchaikovsky's *Romeo and Juliet*, certain episodes are identifiable, but generally the work is a character-study of Macbeth and Lady Macbeth. It is music that stands independently of its programme; its weakness, the reason for its relative neglect, may be that it falls between two stools. It is not so graphic that – as in the case of *Till Eulenspiegel* – the listener demands to know what it is 'about', nor is its thematic invention so compelling that – as in the case of *Don Juan* – the listener does not care what it is about. Yet *Macbeth* is unjustly overlooked. It is not a work of genius but of nascent genius. It repays careful listening.

Macbeth anticipated *Also sprach Zarathustra* in beginning with a fanfare-type motif which acts throughout as a unifying theme. It represents the idea of kingship:

Ex.1

There are two Macbeth themes, identified as such in the score, the first a militaristic, vaulting theme in D minor, the second more subtle in its depiction of regal character flawed by instability (there is a vague similarity in this fine theme to that with which Elgar defines the contradictions in the personality of Shakespeare's Falstaff):

Ex.2

The Macbeth section ended, Strauss goes into A major for Lady Macbeth, the key in which several of his operatic heroines were to move and have their being (Salome and Arabella, for example). To emphasise that he is principally concerned with Lady Macbeth's influence on her husband, Strauss quotes from the play in the score:

> Hie thee hither,
> That I may pour my spirits in thine ear,
> And chastise with the valour of my tongue
> All that impedes thee from the golden round
> Which fate and metaphysical aid doth seem
> To have thee crown'd withal.
>
> (Act I Scene 5)

The future dramatist is audible in the theme for woodwind and strings Strauss devises to portray the feminine allure and sexuality of Lady Macbeth:

Ex.3

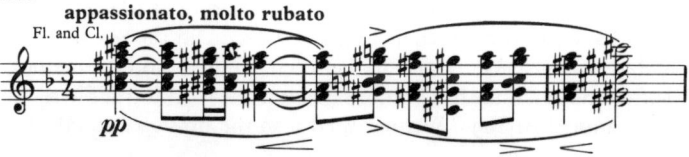

A second theme indicates the conflicting elements in her personality. Having completed the exposition, Strauss begins the development with a dialogue between Macbeth and his wife, the latter gradually assuming dominance. Both are given extra themes in this section, he a romantic figure marked *dolce*, she a serpentine melody which coils round Macbeth so that he agrees to her murderous plans:

Ex.4

Now, after an *accelerando*, comes the first episode with the return and grandiose expansion of Ex. 1 to signify Duncan's arrival at the castle. Lady Macbeth's themes, particularly Ex. 4, are much in evidence in the subsequent passage, before Strauss embarks on a finely constructed symphonic development of the protagonists' main themes, an excellent piece of composition, tautly argued and orchestrated in unmistakable manner – this is post-*Don Juan* Strauss. Throughout this passage Ex. 1 is a binding factor and Lady Macbeth is represented by her more turbulent second theme and by Ex. 4. The climax is the knocking which alarms Macbeth after the murder of Duncan and which leads into the second episode, a brief exchange between Macbeth's first, martial theme and Lady Macbeth's Ex. 4. A second climax is followed by the repetition of the Macbeth exposition from the start of the tone poem. This brief recapitulation ends with the death of Macbeth and his wife, hers being signalled by faltering fragments of Ex. 3. Quiet fanfares – the triumph of Macduff – begin the coda, which is mainly concerned with a final version of the *dolce* figure that stood for the best in Macbeth's character.

It is a reminder of how far we are from the musical world of 1889 that Strauss's father and Bülow should have been disturbed by the dissonances in *Macbeth* and by the 'monstrousness' of its orchestra. But it is clear from *Macbeth* that Strauss, like Wagner and Mahler, did not enlarge the orchestra merely because he wanted to make a huge noise; he wanted a wider, more varied tonal palette, a more intense harmonic expressiveness, the chance for a richer background to solo instruments. One interesting feature of the scoring of *Macbeth* is the use of a bass trumpet, which he added to the score in 1890 as 'the only possible bridge and intermediary between trumpets and trombones' to soften the brass. He had encountered it while working at Bayreuth in the summer of 1899: Wagner used it in the brass section of *The Ring*.

With hindsight, we can see that *Macbeth* is the work of an embryonic opera-composer. The music is at its most alive and compelling in the dramatic conflicts of the characters of Macbeth and his wife; and the ending of the work, from the off-stage side-drum roll and fanfares, is theatrical in conception.

Don Juan, Op.20

After completing *Macbeth*, a work of exceptional talent, Strauss composed *Don Juan*, a work of blazing genius. That he should have crossed this divide in so short a time was due, I believe, not to some sudden maturing and intensifying of his compositional powers but because this was the first of his works which may be called autobiographical. For *Don Juan* read *Richard Strauss*. Thus there is an extra immediacy in the music, a closer identification with the element we now recognise as 'Straussian'. It is tumescent, erotic music, redolent of the passion of a man in his mid-twenties. From the late summer of 1887 Strauss had been giving singing lessons to a young soprano, Pauline de Ahna. He was to marry her in 1894, but it is doubtful if he had more than a professional interest in her until about 1890, two years after the completion of *Don Juan*. The impetus for this work came from his passion for Dora Wihan, whom he had first met in 1883 when she was twenty-three and he was nineteen. Born in Dresden as Dora Weis, she was a pianist and a close friend of Strauss's sister. She married Hanuš Wihan, the cellist, who in November 1883 played in the first performance of Strauss's Cello Sonata and was eventually to be the dedicatee of Dvořák's Cello Concerto. The Wihans' marriage broke up in 1885, but not because of Strauss. For the next four years Strauss and Dora saw each other and corresponded regularly.

The subject of *Don Juan* had suggested itself to Strauss not through any Mozartian connection but after he had seen Paul Heyse's play *Don Juans Ende* in Frankfurt in 1885 and had read Nikolaus Lenau's unfinished verse drama *Don Juan* (published in 1851). First sketches of the tone poem were made in Padua in May 1888; it was completed on 30 September of that year. Strauss conducted the first performance at Weimar on 11 November 1889. Letters to his father describing the rehearsals show that the orchestra enjoyed the new work in spite of its difficulties ('I felt really sorry for the poor horns and trumpets. They blew till they were blue in the face'). The piece was a success.

Don Juan is composed to the same structural design as *Macbeth*. Although some incidents are illustrated, it is more of a psychological study than a representational piece. Lenau's Don Juan is very different from da Ponte's Don Giovanni. Lenau outlines Juan's career, from the vain pleas of his brother, Don Diego, that he should leave his dissolute life and return home to his father, to the duel in which he not unwillingly dies. He depicts a Juan who is deeply discontented because, in his pursuit of the pleasure of the moment, he inflicts lasting harm on those involved. Three quotations from the poem head Strauss's score. In the first Don Juan expresses his philosophy:

Would that I could fly through every place where beauty blossoms . . . and, were it but for a moment, conquer.

The second is from Juan's reply to his brother's warnings:

I keep myself fresh in the service of beauty; . . . The breath of a woman that is as the odour of spring today may perhaps tomorrow oppress me like the air of a dungeon . . . Passion is always and only the new passion, it cannot be carried from this one to that . . . Forth and away, then, to triumphs ever new, so long as youth's fiery pulses race!

In the third quotation, Juan gloomily awaits his fate:

It was a beautiful storm that urged me on; it has spent its passion, and silence now remains . . . The fuel is all consumed and the hearth is cold and dark.

The opening of *Don Juan* is one of the most thrilling and difficult passages in orchestral music. Youth's fiery pulses race here, and no mistake. A flurry on the strings, crowned by ringing trumpet tone, is the perfect transliteration into music of ardour and desire – hedonism in sound. The passage is an assembly of short motifs, a piece of virtuoso invention in itself, allied to inventive brilliance:

Ex.5
Allegro molto con brio

The real first subject follows immediately (Ex. 6 opposite). Throughout this first expository section the constituents of Ex. 5 flit about the score like flashing rapiers. Spurred by this subject-matter, Strauss displays for the first time his mature creative armoury – a command

DON JUAN

Ex.6

of orchestral resource and virtuosity that assaults the ear with its freshness and daring after nearly a century. (Note the novel and effective use of the triangle, borrowed from the *scherzo* of Brahms's Fourth Symphony which Strauss learned intimately at its first performance at Meiningen.)

Next comes Juan's first amatory encounter, more a flirtation than an *amour* to judge from the capricious theme representing the girl:

Ex.7

Yet the episode ends with the first statement, *fortissimo*, of a melody which later is the basis of a more impassioned scene:

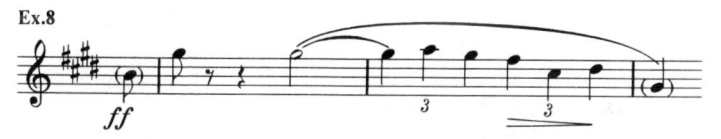

Ex.8

With a motif from Ex. 5, Juan leaves this dalliance and is at once captivated by a new love (woodwind chord). A solo violin makes seductive use of part of Ex. 8, which is then expanded into the work's first 'heavy' love scene. As the ardour subsides, the cellos – first drowsily, then with renewed vigour – play part of Ex. 5, the clarinet catches on – and off races Juan into a development section based chiefly on his own themes, until a new fancy catches his eye and requires a new melody, given urgent intensity by the lower strings:

Ex.9

molto appass.

In this episode the seduction is clearly portrayed, the plaintive (*flebile*) flute representing the woman's weakening resolve against the promptings of another motif from Ex. 5. This woman, whoever she may have been, obviously meant more to Juan than the others; and perhaps it is Strauss's Dora who is here immortalised in music of touching and nostalgic beauty, characterised by this oboe solo:

Ex.10

This poignant melody is given to other wind instruments, sounding elegiac on the horn, but returns repeatedly to the oboe. A contented version of Ex. 9, heard over a background of divided strings, completes the picture of amorous satiety. It is now that one can justify the claim that in this work Strauss became a composer of genius. Instead of merging into a conventional recapitulation, he follows this central 'slow movement' by emulating a comparable passage in the last scene of Wagner's *Die Walküre* and introducing a new Juan motif, the most striking of all. After a surge of violin tone ending in a high trill, four horns proclaim:

Ex.11

So begins the second development section, depicting Juan at a masked ball. The calm loveliness of the oboe's Ex. 10 is converted into anxious, shaken fright as Juan flings himself into new activity. The various motifs of Ex. 5 are interspersed with Ex. 11 to build a carnival atmosphere which owes something to the 'Venusberg' music in Wagner's *Tannhäuser* – this is where the horn players and trumpeters were blue in the face! A glockenspiel adds a further exotic touch. At the height of the festivity – and with a backward glance to Tchaikovsky's *Francesca da Rimini* – Strauss hurls his hero into the abyss. The disillusioned Juan hears fragments of his mistresses' themes, but the first two bars of Ex. 5 hesitantly inaugurate a revival of confidence as Strauss, with concise and dramatic élan, sweeps towards the recapitulation. This, again, focuses solely on Juan themes, not only Exx. 5 and 6 in their various guises but Ex. 11, even more thrilling than before, with the horns a third higher, and ending with a majestic unison for the upper strings and woodwind. In accordance with strict sonata form, the original exposition of Ex. 5 returns. Events move swiftly – there is not a wasted note in this work – and after the recapitulation Strauss ruthlessly kills his hero who, tired of life but with victory in the duel within his grasp, allows himself to be run through by his opponent. The music is now in E minor; a chord on trumpets is the sword-thrust that fells Juan; and his life shivers away on cold tremolandi from the strings. The effect of flagging energy throughout this coda is as skilfully conveyed as is that of superabundant energy at the opening.

In *Don Juan* we hear Strauss exulting in his command of the orchestra and proclaiming his determination to free himself from the fetters of Munich. Whatever it tells us about his love life, it tells us more about his ambition to be a 'progressive' composer. Asked if he was a Wagnerian or a Brahmsian he replied that he was a 'Selfian'. In *Don Juan* he became Straussian.

Tod und Verklärung, Op. 24

Seven days after conducting the first performance of *Don Juan*, Strauss completed the full score of his third tone poem, *Tod und Verklärung*. He began it probably some time in 1888. In a letter to Dora Wihan dated 9 April 1889 he wrote: 'I've finished the sketch of a new tone poem (probable title: *Tod und Verklärung*) and shall probably start the full score after Easter.'

No personal experience is reflected in the 'programme' of this work. The severe illness which threatened Strauss's life did not occur until May 1891, eleven months after *Tod und Verklärung* had had its first performance. Nor had he before 1888 been present at anyone's deathbed. In 1931 he told a correspondent: '*Tod und Verkl.* is purely a product of the imagination . . . It was an idea like any other, probably ultimately the musical need – after *Macbeth* (begins and ends in D minor), *Don Juan* (begins and ends in E minor) – to write a piece that begins in C minor and finishes in C major!' The tone poem was another success for Strauss at its first performance at Eisenach on 21 June 1890, when he conducted. Everything from his pen was now eagerly awaited: *Don Juan* had made him the leading German composer of his generation, and his fame was spreading. Ritter was particularly enthusiastic about *Tod und Verklärung*. He wrote a poem about its content which Strauss copied into the autograph score and caused to be printed in the programme of the first two performances. When the work was published, another and longer poem by Ritter was printed in the score. Nevertheless the best account of the work's programme was given by Strauss in 1895 in a letter to Friedrich von Hausegger:

. . . the idea occurred to me to represent the death of a person who had striven for the highest artistic goals, therefore very possibly an artist, in a tone poem. The sick man lies in bed asleep, breathing heavily and irregularly; agreeable dreams charm a smile onto his features in spite of his suffering; his sleep becomes lighter; he wakens; once again he is racked by terrible pain, his limbs shake with fear – as the attack draws to a close and the pain subsides he reflects on his past life, his childhood passes before him, his youth with its striving, its passions, and then, while the pain resumes, the fruit of his path through life appears to him, the idea, the Ideal which he has tried to realise, to represent in his art, but which he has been unable to perfect, because it was not for any human being to perfect it. The hour of death approaches, the soul leaves the body, in order to find perfected in the most glorious form in the eternal cosmos that which he could not fulfil here on earth.

In recent years *Tod und Verklärung* has slipped in critical estimation from the high place it formerly occupied. The opinion that Strauss was incapable of invading the deeper or spiritual realms of music has become a commonplace in discussion of his work. Sublimity is a fine word, but if it is to be applied only to art in which there is a fundamentally religious impulse, this becomes an unacceptable limitation. In truth, no composer can convey the kind of transfiguration implied by eternity, since no one knows what is involved. So judgements of this work based on Strauss's alleged failure to rise to celestial heights are worthless. He was not, in any case, trying to convey a Christian idea of the after-life in his *Verklärung*. He was an unbeliever, and was careful in his 'programme' to refer to space – the 'eternal cosmos' – rather than to any religious concept of eternity. The only applicable criterion is whether the music achieves an inventiveness, of form and beauty, to match the composer's aspiration. If you consider the *Idealism* theme (on which the *Transfiguration* section is based) to be banal, then you will find the work a failure (having, I trust, taken into account the quality of performance and interpretation). But those who admire the *Idealism* theme – and no one, so far as I know, has ever criticised its movingly apposite effectiveness when Strauss quotes it in 'Im Abendrot' in the *Vier letzte Lieder* – may still find *Tod und Verklärung* a slight falling-back after *Don Juan* because of its lack of vivid dramatic characterisation. There is no lack of atmospheric tone-painting, no shortage of inspired harmonic modulations, but there is a relative slackening of the electric tension generated by thematic contrasts.

In the introduction Strauss leads the listener into the sick-room, its atmosphere oppressive and anxious. An asymmetrical rhythmical motif – faltering pulse or laboured breathing – is shared between strings and timpani; weary sighs are heaved by the strings and the flutes. The dreams which bring a smile to the dying man's face begin on the harp, followed by a descending phrase on flute and a rising one on oboe – perhaps it is not so much a dream as the kindly ministration of a nurse. The introductory music returns, until the harp again prefaces the next 'dream', an oboe phrase representing the innocence of childhood and sounding even more sweetly youthful on solo violin. A skilful polyphony of all these motifs closes this prelude, which may have suggested something to Elgar for *The Dream of Gerontius*, although both composers are indebted to the prelude to Act III of *Tristan und Isolde* and to that to Act I of *Parsifal*.

A drum-beat changes mood and tempo for the *allegro*, in which the sufferer's agonies are conveyed, though with considerable restraint. New themes are heard here, but to describe them as the first and second subject is perhaps stretching analytical licence. The work's main theme, the *Idealism* motif, has not yet been heard, though first hints of it come towards the end of this *allegro* (Ex. 12 overleaf).

Ex.12

espr.

Violins on a high D close the *allegro*. The development begins in G major, Strauss's favourite key for youth and innocence, the key of Daphne in her opera, of Zdenka in *Arabella* and of the Naiads in *Ariadne auf Naxos*. The childhood theme, with pendants, returns on the flute; sumptuous writing for strings and other felicities of scoring suggest the future opera composer by their illuminative detail. Youthful ardour and impetuosity – whether as lover or man of action is not clear – bring a modulation to E flat and a theme for horns and strings which sounds new but is a compound of two earlier fragments. From this arises an *appassionato* passage in B major, ardent enough for a love scene but perhaps more illustrative of a generally passionate enthusiasm for life. Its exciting course is interrupted twice by trombones and timpani recalling the palpitations of the sick-room, but it culminates in three successive and widely separated statements of the *Idealism* theme (Ex. 12), each in a different key and each more elaborate than its predecessor. Strauss regarded this melody as the main theme of the work. He wrote that '*Tod und Verklärung* makes the main theme its point of culmination, and does not state it until the middle'.

After the third statement, the recapitulation of the introduction begins. The 'agony' section is curtailed and death comes on the tam-tam. Now, out of the mysterious darkness, the *Idealism* theme emerges slowly and almost unrecognisably on horns and higher wind instruments. The strings reach to a high G and Ex. 12 returns in its transfiguration in C major. With initial restraint and intensifying harmonic richness the coda builds towards the final statement of Ex. 12. When the work was still quite new, an English critic, Arthur Johnstone, described this apotheosis as 'too well done not to have been sincerely felt'. Only an insincere performance invalidates this judgement.

Till Eulenspiegel, Op. 28

After the completion of *Tod und Verklärung* five years passed before Strauss began his next tone poem. For several reasons these five years from 1889 to 1894 were among the leanest for composition Strauss ever experienced. He was kept busy in his opera-conducting post at Weimar and, in addition, the success of *Don Juan* and *Tod und Verklärung* led to his being in demand as a guest conductor of his own works throughout Germany. Since 1887 he had been working intermittently on the libretto of his first opera, *Guntram*, and he began to compose the music in 1892. In May 1891 he was seriously ill with pneumonia and exactly a year later had pleurisy and bronchitis. In November 1892 he left for a prolonged convalescence in Greece and Egypt. While abroad he worked on the music of *Guntram* and sketched libretti for two other operas (which, like his 1892 sketches for the libretto of a *Don Juan* opera, came to naught). He stayed abroad until the midsummer of 1893, returning to his Weimar duties in October. He conducted the world première of Humperdinck's *Hänsel und Gretel* there at Christmas. In February 1894 his mentor Bülow died; a month later Strauss became secretly engaged to Pauline de Ahna, the soprano whom he had taught since 1887 and who was a member of the Weimar Opera; on 10 May he conducted the first performance of *Guntram*, with Pauline singing the role of the heroine Freihild; in July he conducted for the first time at Bayreuth (*Tannhäuser*); and on 10 September he and Pauline were married. Three weeks later he took up his new post as Kapellmeister in Munich. Apart from some occasional pieces written for Weimar court galas, Strauss's only non-operatic compositions between 1889 and 1894 were two Lenau settings in 1891 and the four marvellous songs of Op. 27, composed in May and September 1894 as a wedding-present for Pauline.

In the autumn of 1893 Strauss began to write the libretto for a one-act opera to be called *Till Eulenspiegel and the Burghers of Schilda*. Again, an autobiographical element was present. Schilda exists only in German folklore and Strauss depicted the burghers as grotesque philistines. Till was 'the fruitless sceptic, the laughing philosopher'. In other words, Strauss was trying to dramatise his own relationship with the 'stuffy' musical philistines of Weimar and Munich, a plan he carried out some years later in the opera *Feuersnot*. At some point in 1894 he abandoned the *Till* project, realising he lacked poetic gifts as a librettist. Instead he used Till as the subject for a tone poem. There is no evidence, and little likelihood, that any music for the opera had been sketched, so the orchestral masterpiece owes nothing but its title to operatic origins. Nor had Till's exploits in the opera much resemblance to the 'merry pranks', or 'gleeful exploits', of the rogue concert audiences have grown to love.

Strauss was probably drawn to Till because, being a voracious reader, he had seen one of the several new editions of stories about him published, with etchings, at this date in Germany. There was a real Till, who died (in his bed) near Lübeck in 1350. The anecdotes about him began to be printed 150 years later. They celebrated the points scored by this lower-class individual against the upper class and the authorities; they tell of his enforced journeying from place to place in order to elude retribution for his misdemeanours: he was always outwitting scholars or judges, playing practical jokes, or being witty at the expense of the powerful. The Till of Strauss's opera libretto would have had none of his orchestral counterpart's variety and much less of Strauss himself.

Two factors are dominant in their contribution to this delightful work, in which a Haydnesque humour returned to European music: the orchestration is bold and innovative in the limits to which it takes individual instruments, particularly the woodwind family; and the choice of a sonata rondo (A-B-A-C-A-B-A) as the form in which to illustrate Till's adventures, with his own themes as the recurring 'A' subject, is inspired.

The gentle opening for strings establishes the quasi-fairy-tale nature of *Till Eulenspiegel* – 'Once upon a time . . .' – and at the seventeenth bar the solo horn plays the once-heard-never-forgotten theme with which Strauss at a stroke immortalised his knavish folk-hero:

Ex.13

The subtle hesitancy of the first part of this theme suggests that Till is not too sure how he will be received into our company. But the theme is worked up to a climax after which the D clarinet – its use is a major feature of the score – introduces the second Till theme ('He was a wicked goblin' was Strauss's identification of its import), though equally striking is the pendant chord for three oboes and cor anglais:

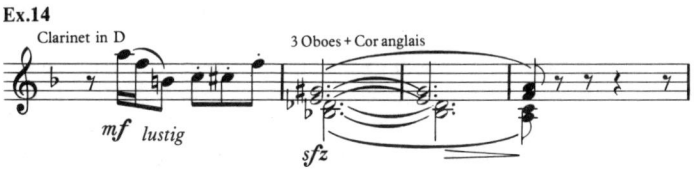

Ex.14

'Up to new tricks' is Strauss's label on the next section, a reference to his own methods as much as to anything Till does. In what amounts to an exposition he makes play with various aspects of Ex. 13, the texture light, the wit scintillating. A lightly scored *grazioso* linking passage – 'Just wait, you fainthearts' – precedes the next programmatic episode, which begins with an upward swoop on all the clarinets from the bass to the D and a crash of cymbals, as Till rides on horseback through the market-women, scattering pots and pans and causing general chaos. He escapes in seven-league boots – trombones' augmentation of Ex. 13. There is a pause. Till is hidden in a mouse's hole and peeps out (woodwind) to see if all is safe. He emerges in disguise as a priest, oozing 'unction and morality' on violas and bassoons in what is the second subject – the 'B' – of the rondo. As Strauss put it, 'the knave peeps out [of his disguise] at the big toe', this being conveyed musically by a flash of Ex. 14 on the D clarinet and fragments of Ex. 13 elsewhere. In the midst of his sermon, though, Till has a nasty turn – on muted horns, trumpets and five muted solo violins in four-part chromatic harmony – when 'because of his mockery of religion, he feels a sudden horror of his end'. This is one of several passages in the tone poem when Strauss, by the simplest means, injects a medieval atmosphere into the music.

The premonitions vanish, and with a glissando descent on solo violin Till, in his form as Ex. 14, comes over amorous, on clarinets, for his adventure as a gallant, 'exchanging dainty courtesies with pretty girls'. Soon even Ex. 13 succumbs to the need to woo, in this version for D clarinet and first violins, supported by richer harmonies (Ex. 15 overleaf).

Ex.15

liebeglühend
Vl. 1, Flutes and Cl. in D

espr.

No joy, though. He is jilted and, through an angry Ex. 13 on four horns, 'vows revenge on the whole human race'. His fury abates as Ex. 14 returns on D clarinet, suggesting that a new prank has occurred to him. He meets some philistines, their views expounded by three bassoons, double bassoon and bass clarinet. Till has some questions for them – Ex. 13 in yet another rhythmical manifestation – which cause consternation. Their bafflement by his 'whopping theses' is followed by Till's (Ex. 14) derision shrieked out on trumpet, woodwind and violins, culminating in a giant trill. This is followed by one of the most inspired moments in the work: the savage mood evaporates into Till's jaunty whistling of a street ditty as he strolls away. This ends the 'C' section of the rondo. Till's whistling dies away to be succeeded by a lightly scored passage marked *Schnell und schattenhaft* ('fast and shadowy'). Strauss again marks time with a genial, unprogrammatic episode which includes the *piano* return of Ex. 13, first on the F horn, then on the D, and a fanfare-like version of the same theme. Again the texture is admirably lucid, the *scherzando* mood of the work skilfully maintained. As horns and trumpets blare forth the theme of Till's sermon, Strauss quickly brings the narrative to its inevitable climax: a charge of blasphemy.

Till's trial begins with a low roll on the side-drum. He is unmoved and 'whistles nonchalantly' (Ex. 14), but the majesty of the law penetrates his indifference and the premonition he had after preaching his sermon returns in agitated form. He is condemned to death, the sentence taking the form of a descending major seventh ('der Tod'). He is to be hanged, and the music assumes the atmosphere (and almost the notes) of the execution in the 'March to the Scaffold' in Berlioz's *Symphonie fantastique*. The D clarinet ascends rapidly to its higher A flat, is suspended, and then slowly descends. Till's last convulsions are the shakes of a flute. But this is not the end. A gentle Epilogue recalls the work's fairy-tale opening, as if to remind us, before he scampers away, that Till was not such a bad fellow.

TILL EULENSPIEGEL

This was to be the last of Strauss's short tone poems. He was always at his best when he could bring humour into his work, and the sheer ebullience of *Till* never slackens. The music uncannily illustrates its 'programme', but if Strauss had merely entitled it Rondo for Orchestra it would still have commanded a rapid and permanent place in the repertoire as one of his merriest orchestral pranks. No one should fail to hear Strauss's own remarkable recording of *Till*. It has tenderness, but also a venom that eludes most conductors. Where others provide a bee-sting, Strauss provides a scorpion's.

Also sprach Zarathustra, Op. 30

Strauss came to know Nietzsche's writings while he was in Egypt in 1892. The philosopher's 'polemics against the Christian religion in particular struck a chord in me, and reading him strengthened and corroborated the antipathy which I had unconsciously felt since my fifteenth year for this religion which frees its believers of responsibility for their own actions [through confession]'. It was this antipathy to religion which had led to his break with Ritter over the last act of *Guntram*. Ritter, a devout Roman Catholic, never forgave Strauss for his revision of the last act. Originally the hero Guntram was to confess his guilt to his religious sect and accept the punishment they awarded him. But, under Nietzsche's influence, Strauss revised this to allow Guntram to reject society and the authority of his sect and be answerable only to himself. It reads like a storm in a teacup today, but it was earth-shaking a century ago. And all it really meant was that Strauss the musician was determined to go his own way and be answerable only to his own artistic conscience.

Also sprach Zarathustra, Nietzsche's prose-poem, was completed in 1885. Nietzsche used the Persian mystic Zoroaster, who lived *circa* 600 BC, as spokesman for his own philosophy and views on war, chastity, women, religion and science. The prophet retreats from human society into a mountain cave, returning intermittently to give his disciples the benefit of his solitary musings. One of the principal planks in his manifesto for mankind is the theory of 'rule by the best', by the *Übermensch* or Superman: 'Man is a thing to be surmounted . . . Man is great in that he is a bridge not a goal . . . The Superman shall be the meaning of the earth.' This theory rapidly became tarnished by events when, twice within the space of forty years, German militarism plunged Europe into war. The effort of formulating it causes Zarathustra nervous exhaustion, but during his convalescence, in Nietzsche's book, he becomes a transfigured being, his philosophy gushing forth in poetry, with references to mountains and sunrises, to the dancing of girls and the tolling of the midnight bell, and with invocations to the Will and Eternity. Into this section, too, is inserted the eleven-line poem beginning 'O Mensch, gib Acht' ('O Man, take heed') which Mahler commandeered for a movement in his Third Symphony. It was this romantic imagery, expressed in ornate language, that attracted composers to Nietzsche. It is surely no coincidence that three of the masters of post-Wagnerian musical romanticism seized upon *Also sprach Zarathustra* almost simultaneously and independently – Strauss from 1894 to 1896, Mahler from 1895 to 1896 and Delius in 1898.

Barbara W. Tuchman, in her brilliant and absorbing book *The Proud Tower*, first published in 1966, depicts Strauss as the musical counterpart of the Kaiser, in order to fit her theory, borrowed from Romain Rolland, of 'Neroism in the air' of Europe at the turn of the century. She asserts that Strauss was 'a convinced believer in *Übermensch*'. Historians like to see artists as symbols of the *Zeitgeist*, but they tend to look no deeper than the surface. To equate Strauss with the spirit of Wilhelmine militarism is as misleading as it is to equate Elgar with English jingoism. Miss Tuchman cites no documentary evidence in support of her assertion. Strauss's admiration was for Nietzsche's literary prowess, not for his philosophy. He wrote in 1946 of the 'aesthetic enjoyment' he derived from *Also sprach Zarathustra*. Fifty years earlier, at the time of his composition's first Berlin performance, he stated categorically that he did not intend 'to write philosophical music . . . I meant rather to convey in music an idea of the evolution of the human race from its origin, through the various phases of development, religious as well as scientific, up to Nietzsche's idea of the *Übermensch*. The whole symphonic poem is intended as my homage to the genius of Nietzsche.'

There is no 'plot' in Strauss's *Also sprach Zarathustra*, no graphic description of incidents as in *Till Eulenspiegel*. This is a tone poem about abstract ideas, but Strauss gave it dramatic and musical conflict by basing it on the alternation and opposition between two remote tonalities, B representing Man and C representing Nature. Although he chose eight of Nietzsche's chapter headings as guides to the musical episodes, he described the whole work as 'freely after Nietzsche' to give himself an escape route from too close an identification with what music could achieve as a depiction of literature. The work is Nietzschean in its outlines; its inner parts and detail and its essential spirit are Straussian. The closest musical approximation to Nietzsche is Delius's *A Mass of Life*. Delius regarded Strauss's *Zarathustra* as a failure. From where he was looking, no doubt it is; but the quick-wittedness of Strauss's invention, the virtuosity of the scoring, the economical nature of its organic structure and the distinctiveness of its harmonic spectrum give the work a strength and beauty which have long since superseded Nietzsche. Strauss himself realised this. After its final Frankfurt rehearsal he wrote to his wife that it was 'glorious – by far the most important of all my pieces, the most perfect in form, the richest in content and the most individual in colour . . . The climaxes are immense and scored!!! Faultlessly scored . . .' If this sounds dangerously like self-satisfaction, it happened to be true at the time – and it is also perhaps the excited reaction of the professional conductor rather than the smugness of the creator.

The very first musical idea which found its way into *Zarathustra* was sketched in Weimar in February 1894. Then a note in his diary for 9 July 1895 showed that he was 'plotting' *Zarathustra*: 'Thought about a new tone poem: Contemplation. Experience. Recognition. Worship. Doubting. Despair.' He got down to the project in earnest on 7 December 1895, completing the short score on 17 July 1896. Work on the full score stretched from 4 February 1896 to 24 August 1896. These are the titles of the sections after the famous and magnificent opening sunrise (Strauss's words for it were: 'The sun rises. The individual enters the world or the world enters the individual'): *Von den Hinterweltlern (Of the Backworldsmen)*; *Von der grossen Sehnsucht (Of the great longing)*; *Von den Freuden und Leidenschaften (Of joys and passions)*; *Das Grablied (The Song of the Grave)*; *Von der Wissenschaft (Of Science)*; *Der Genesende (The Convalescent)*; *Das Tanzlied (The Dance Song)*; and *Nachtwandlerlied (Song of the Night Wanderer)*. The orchestra includes quadruple woodwind, six horns, four trumpets, three trombones, two tubas, two harps and an organ. The scoring is remarkably translucent – when Strauss doubled instruments he achieved something finer than a turgid thickening of the texture (as did Mahler).

It is the organ, holding a C in the primeval depths for four bars, which begins the tone poem. From this arises the Nature-motif – C-G-C – played by four trumpets and followed by dramatic alternations of major and minor, with timpani beating out thunderous triplets. This compelling passage, so cleverly appropriated in 1968 by Stanley Kubrick for his space film *2001*, reaches a climax that ends with the organ holding the last note. Man comes on the scene in B minor:

Ex.16

This is reached by way of some ominous groping on tremolando strings, the 'Backworldsmen' evidently in search of religion for, after Ex. 16, muted horns play the plainchant Credo theme as an ironic comment. This merges into one of Strauss's first sumptuous orchestral melodisings, with the strings divided into sixteen parts and a gentle organ accompaniment. Here we encounter a characteristic Straussian hallmark, the modulation into a distant key by means of a harmonic 'side-slip'. Cor anglais and solo viola lead into the 'Great Longing' and the return of B as the principal key, soon to be opposed by the C major of the Nature-motif in a polytonal passage which caused a considerable stir when the work was new. Religion, this time represented by the plainchant Magnificat on the organ, is swept aside by an upward-thrusting theme on the lower strings which launches the 'Joys and Passions' section.

The fervour of this episode is suddenly chilled by the trombones, which introduce a new theme:

Ex.17

Arthur Seidl, writing an analysis of this tone poem (with Strauss's blessing) in 1898, labelled this theme 'Disgust' – Zarathustra's protest against sensual indulgence. Ernest Newman derided the very notion that music could express disgust. Nevertheless, the theme is

ALSO SPRACH ZARATHUSTRA

apt for its purpose, especially when regarded as part of the work's closely-integrated musical structure, through its relationship to the opposing keys of B and C. In 'The Song of the Grave', the B minor tonality gives a muted colouring to the texture, misty and veiled, with Ex. 16 trying to regain supremacy. The Nature-motif returns on a solo trumpet in a brilliant climax before the gloom obscures this shaft of light – and Strauss shows his grasp of 'Science' with a deliberately erudite fugue-theme based on the Nature and Man motifs and employing all twelve notes of the chromatic scale, arranged in five different keys in three rhythms. But this sombre mood is not allowed to last for long. Ex. 16 is up and away into the 'Convalescent' scherzo. Although Ex. 17 makes several efforts to reassert scientific seriousness, it doesn't stand a chance against the exuberance of Man's spirit and is eventually transformed into Till Eulenspiegel on E flat clarinet. An orgy of trills and trumpet-calls takes the music – by way of repetitions of the Nature-motif – to the brink of the 'Dance Song', the dance of the Superman, in C major.

The Dance is Strauss's first use of a Viennese waltz – solo violin *mit Schwung* ('with swing') and a playful oboe – at a crucial point in a composition. Here is incontrovertible proof that Strauss gives no hostages to Tuchmanite theories of his sympathy for the Superman philosophy. The Superman waltzing on the dance-floor! The irrelevance is a captivating example of deflationary Bavarian humour. The waltz theme, incidentally, is another skilful combination of Nature and Man. The first three notes of the oboe theme are the Nature-motif, the other four belong to Ex. 16:

Ex.18

Ingratiating scoring for strings in seventeen parts and two harps is eventually brushed aside by a return of the dithyrambic dance music from the 'Convalescent' episode and the start of a magnificently constructed development section in which the Nature-motif and Man's theme (Ex. 16), with their opposing tonalities constantly displacing each other, are built up vehemently as the dance whirls on in spite of violent interruptions of its progress by the 'Disgust' motif (Ex. 17). A triumphant statement of Ex. 16 takes the dance to its C major climax with Nature-motif and Ex. 18 combined. But it is Ex. 17 that holds sway ferociously as the Midnight Bell tolls in the 'Night Wanderer's Song'. In the poem Zarathustra expounds the victory of joy over woe in a strange mixture of awe and exultation. In the tone poem the bell's strokes slowly vanquish the power of Ex. 17. The tonality slips from the glare of C into the soft nocturnal radiance of B major. Man's theme, Ex. 16, is heard as a counter-melody on bassoons, the 'Disgust' motif has one final stab, but conflict becomes a distant memory as the enveloping harmonies of the *pianissimo* coda remove its traces – except for the basic unresolved conflict of Man and Nature, B and C. The Nature-motif in C on trombones and double basses alternates with remote high woodwind chords of B major, and it is Nature, on pizzicato cellos and basses, that is the last sound we hear.

Whereas in *Till Eulenspiegel* and *Don Quixote* knowledge of the events portrayed adds a dimension to enjoyment of the music, in *Also sprach Zarathustra* it is unnecessary to keep even a vague memory of a 'programme' as one listens. It is no coincidence that the popularity of *Zarathustra* has increased in recent years – and this began before *2001: A Space Odyssey*. The expert orchestras and conductors of today are not intimidated by its difficulties; they relish the challenge and revel in the scoring. Audiences, I suspect, neither know nor care about Nietzsche and Zarathustra. They hear this colourful, exciting, inventive music, ecstatic, compelling and witty by turns, they recognise its melodic vitality, and for them it becomes *Also sprach Richard Strauss*.

Don Quixote, Op. 35

In October 1896 the Strausses went to Florence for a holiday. On the 11th Strauss wrote in his diary: 'First idea for an orchestral piece: Don Quichote, mad, free variations on a knightly theme.' This was a busy time for Strauss. In addition to his operatic conducting in Munich, he travelled abroad in the early months of 1897 as guest conductor of his own works and toured widely with the Munich Intendant, Ernst von Possart, for whom he had in February 1897 completed the melodrama for speaker and piano, *Enoch Arden*, a setting of Tennyson's poem in a translation by Adolph Strodtmann.

DON QUIXOTE

(Strauss was with Possart in Stuttgart on 12 April when he received news of the birth of his son Franz after Pauline's difficult and dangerous confinement.) In November 1896 he had made some notes for a new opera (abandoned), *Die Schildbürger*; five days later he wrote some ballet music for a *Singspiel* based on Goethe's *Lila* (this too was abandoned). More fruitful was his songwriting, for this was one of his great lyric periods, inspired by his happiness with Pauline. In December 1896 and January 1897 he composed the third and fourth (*Hymnus* and *Pilgers Morgenlied*) of his Op. 33 songs with orchestra. In the spring of 1897 he composed two of his wonderful unaccompanied part-songs, *Hymne* and *Der Abend*, Op. 34, the choral equivalents of the virtuoso orchestral passages in *Zarathustra*, masterpieces which are still too little known and appreciated.

Hymne was completed on 25 April, but on 16 April Strauss had entered in his diary: 'Symphonic poem *Held und Welt* begins to take shape; as satyr play to accompany it – *Don Quichote*.' *Held und Welt* (*Hero and World*) was finally to become *Ein Heldenleben* (*A Hero's Life*). For Strauss these two works were indissolubly linked in his creative imagination and they were conceived alongside each other, as his diary entries show: in June and July he wrote that he was busy on *Don Quichote* (the spelling he favoured at this time) and *Held und Welt* or, as it temporarily became, 'The Heroic Symphony'. His view on the matter was expressed in 1898 to Gustav Kogel, director of the Frankfurt Museum concerts, when he wrote that '*Don Quixote* and *Heldenleben* are conceived so much as immediate pendants that, in particular, *Don Q.* is only fully and entirely comprehensible at the side of *Heldenleben*'. The listener, who has not been privy to the inner workings of Strauss's musical mind, will not find this an easy or convincing theory, but the works certainly depict heroism in two contrasted aspects.

Strauss composed the ending of *Don Quixote* on 22 July 1897 when some of the preceding sections still remained to be written. He began the full score on 12 August and finished it on the morning of 29 December, a long span by his standards. His sketchbooks reveal that, alongside themes and their working-out, he wrote out details of the 'programme' as a kind of *aide-mémoire*, for example: '. . . Don Q. unfolds his vision of peace to him; when S. [Sancho Panza] again expresses his doubts after this, Don Q. becomes enraged, whereupon S. holds his tongue and goes to bed; then cello solo, vigil, lament.'

Not the least of the inspirations in this marvellous composition –

the greatest of the tone poems, in my opinion, and one of the very greatest of Strauss's works – is the use of variation-form to depict Quixote's fantastic adventures, which Strauss selected from Cervantes's novel with much skill, choosing his own order for them and altering events when it suited his musical purpose. (We may note in passing that, a year later, an English composer also chose variation-form as the means of characterising the quirks, some of them quixotic, of his close friends.) Strauss himself described *Don Quixote* as 'the battle of *one* theme against a nullity' and said that in it he had taken 'variation form *ad absurdum* and showered tragicomic persiflage upon it'. The mixture of humour and pathos – the essence of the operatic Strauss – is in *Don Quixote* allied to orchestration which in its flights of fancy is unsurpassed for aptness of invention. All Strauss's virtues are exemplified here; his failings are never in evidence. The score shares its imaginative vision, its power to penetrate to the vitals of music, with the poignant tenderness and pain of the finest episodes in Mahler's and Elgar's symphonies. It makes nonsense of misgivings about and preoccupations with programme music: it is as graphic and vivid as any pictorial illustrations, and as pure musical art it is self-contained.

Strauss's synopsis is as follows:

Introduction: From much reading of romances of chivalry, Don Quixote loses his wits and decides to become a knight errant himself.

Theme: Don Quixote, the knight of the sorrowful countenance (solo cello); Sancho Panza (bass clarinet, tenor tuba and solo viola).

Var. 1: The strange pair ride out wearing the favours of the fair Dulcinea of Toboso; adventure with the windmills.

Var. 2: Victory over the army of the great emperor Alifanfaron (battle against the herd of sheep).

Var. 3: Conversation between knight and squire: Sancho's demands, questions and adages, the knight's precepts, pacifications and promises.

Var. 4: Unfortunate adventure with a procession of penitents.

Var. 5: Don Quixote's vigil over his weapons. Pours out his heart to the distant Dulcinea.

Var. 6: Meeting with a peasant girl, who Sancho tells his master is Dulcinea under an enchanter's spell.

Var. 7: Ride through the air.

Var. 8: Ill-starred voyage on the enchanted boat (barcarole).

Var. 9: Battle against the supposed enchanters, two little priests on their mules.

Var. 10: Single combat with the Knight of the Shining Moon. Don Quixote struck to the ground, bids farewell to his arms and returns home, with the intention of becoming a shepherd.

Finale: Having recovered his senses, he decides to spend his remaining days in meditation. Don Quixote's death.

DON QUIXOTE

The work is scored for a large orchestra (though not as large as *Zarathustra*) with six horns, two tubas and wind machine. Don Quixote is represented for most though not all of the time by the solo cello – Strauss intended the part to be played by the leader of the orchestral cellos, but it is so difficult and demanding that it is often played by a virtuoso soloist as if the work were a concerto. To hear such a cellist as Paul Tortelier in the part – he even looks like Quixote while he plays it – is to experience an extra degree of artistry, but there is no doubt that the original intention is more satisfactory, especially in blending with the Sancho Panza instruments, notably the viola.

Don Quixote begins with an introduction in which the knight's principal themes are expounded, though not in the form in which they become the subject for the variations. There are three, each a brilliant invention. The first – 'knightly and *galant*' – is a little woodwind flourish which has almost an apologetic air about it:

Ex.19

The second is a Straussian fingerprint to be found in *Guntram* and in *Till Eulenspiegel*. Here it signifies courteousness. It is played by violins, accompanied by horns and bassoons:

Ex.20

For the third theme Strauss again makes potent use of harmonic side-slips, in this case illustrating Quixote's delusional tendencies:

Ex.21

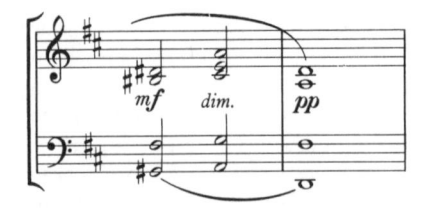

It is this theme, constantly altered, that shows us Quixote absorbed in chivalric romances and dreaming of a lady – eventually incarnated as Dulcinea – to whom to dedicate his deeds. She is enshrined in one of Strauss's loveliest themes, an oboe solo accompanied by harp and two rear desks of muted violins:

Ex.22

Only a composer whose natural talent was for delineation of character could have invented a melody which so perfectly captures idealised, dream-like Woman, scarcely of flesh and blood. After trumpet fanfares – for Quixote is already imagining the need to protect her – the music becomes increasingly complex, the counterpoint a myriad strands, as the old man's reading fills his brain with ever-wilder schemes until violent discords mark the toppling of his reason. As Quixote sets forth, Strauss at last gives the solo cello a composite version of the Quixote themes. The knight's servant Sancho Panza has his own three themes, one for bass clarinet and tenor tuba, the second a garrulous affair for the solo viola, and the third, also for viola, like an epigram.

It is scarcely necessary to follow the adventures (variations) in detail. The instrumental felicities are numerous and unstaling – Quixote and Sancho riding off together (solo cello and bass clarinet) with the Dulcinea theme streaming above them on the violins like a banner; the famous encounter (in Var. 2) with the herd of sheep, imitated to the life by flutter-tonguing woodwind and brass, followed by the shepherd's piping of a theme that will be heard again in *Ein Heldenleben*; the two-part Var. 3 which begins with a *scherzo*-like conversation between knight and servant and ends with Quixote's enraptured vision of the world of chivalry, expressed in one of Strauss's rich, impassioned and sumptuous orchestral cantilenas (based on Ex. 19), ranging from the tonic of F sharp to the distant shores of G natural and B flat, the forerunner of similar episodes in the operas *Die Frau ohne Schatten* and *Die Liebe der Danae*. Sancho brings his master down to earth for the knockabout adventure with the penitents whom Quixote attacks in the mistaken belief that their statue of the Virgin is an abducted maiden. Sancho's joy on discovering that Quixote has not been killed is succeeded by Var. 5, which Elgar would undoubtedly have called an interlude. It shows Quixote keeping vigil over his armour in a moonlit courtyard and is a recitative-like meditation for solo cello based on the Dulcinea theme (Ex. 22) accompanied for most of the variation by other cellos.

After this exquisite and elevated point of repose, Strauss returns to comedy with the bucolic episode of the peasant girl whom Sancho passes off as Dulcinea. Quixote's bewilderment when the lass flees from his salute (Ex. 20) is shown by an apposite use of Ex. 21 with its shifting chromatic harmony. For the hoax flight through the air in Var. 7, Strauss frankly revels in his illusionist powers – wind machine, harp glissandi and flutter-tonguing flutes. But, as Norman Del Mar has pointed out in the first volume of his huge study,[1] a continuous pedal D betrays the real state of affairs: the toy horse is firmly fixed to the ground.

The three last variations form the work's finale and move swiftly. The pair's rescue from drowning when their boat is wrecked merges into the attack by Quixote on the two monks, whose priestly conversation is most amusingly parodied by two unaccompanied bassoons. This petty battle is followed (Var. 10) by the more serious contest with the Knight of the Shining Moon, the violence of the full orchestra pitted against the solo cello. Suddenly the musical fantasising evaporates and Strauss enters the realm of high personal

[1] *Richard Strauss, a critical commentary on his life and works* (London, 1962).

tragedy as Quixote decides to return home. Funereal drum-beats underpin the sensation of collapse in the orchestra's imperious processional elegy. The discord from the Introduction is again the climax, but now it is resolved, for Quixote's reason is returning. Perhaps he will become a shepherd – the *Heldenleben* pastoral theme returns on cor anglais – but this idea is swept aside by a brief resumption of the funereal tread, with Ex. 21 at its core. The discord sounds again, but is banished by soft, high chords in clear and simple harmony – the restoration of sanity. Strauss's epilogue is tender and pathetic. Quixote is dying. The solo cello sings forth with a new version of the principal theme, gently recalls all the Quixote themes in their original form, and expires on a dying fall. Ex. 21 on clarinets and strings ends this masterpiece of romantic art.

Ein Heldenleben, Op. 40

Early progress on this tone poem has been charted above. Sustained work on it began in the summer of 1898, after Strauss had given in his notice to the Munich Opera and signed a contract to become Hofkapellmeister, alongside Karl Muck, at the Berlin Opera. In his diary entries for April, May and June he still refers to working on his 'Eroica', but by 18 July the real title had been decided for he wrote, 'The battle in *Heldenleben* finished'. It was on 23 July that he wrote a famous letter to the publisher Eugen Spitzweg, the ironic tone of which has been missed by some commentators anxious to see Strauss only in an unfavourable light:

As Beethoven's *Eroica* is so very unpopular with our conductors and therefore is seldom performed nowadays, I am now composing, in order to meet a pressing need, a big tone poem entitled *Heldenleben* (true, it has no funeral march, but it *is* in E flat major and has lots of horns, which are of course well versed in heroism) . . .

He finished the composition sketch on 30 July and began to orchestrate fully on 2 August. The full score was completed on 1 December but, as will be seen, more work was still to be done. As in the case of *Don Quixote* he wrote brief summaries against individual motifs, both to remind him where he had reached and to clarify the 'programme'. Thus:

As Adagio the longing for peace, after the battle with the world. Flight into solitude, the idyll.

EIN HELDENLEBEN

And:

After the love scene, the envious and the critics cease to be heard. He remains immersed in D flat major . . . He speaks ever more softly, offers ever more, the indolence remains the same. Then he is seized by disgust, withdraws entirely into the idyll, in order to live only for his thoughts, his wishes, the unfolding of his own personality in quiet and contemplation. Autumnal forest – resignation at the side of the beloved – music dies away warmheartedly, several pages like the last close of the love scene/duet.

None of Strauss's orchestral works, not even *Also sprach Zarathustra*, has led to more misconceptions than *Ein Heldenleben*. With the assumption, not entirely justifiable, that the Hero was Strauss himself, there went the corollary that here was typical German post-Bismarckian self-aggrandisement, here again in music was Nietzsche's superman. Those sections which are autobiographical refer to Strauss's love-life and to his career as a conductor. His adversaries are not military forces, even though amusingly depicted as if they were, but music critics. The Hero's works of peace are quotations from his own works – with what else should he confound the critics? He told Willi Schuh, his biographer, in 1946, 'Of course I didn't engage in battles myself, but I could express the works of peace only by using themes of my own.' The Hero's Companion (*Gefährtin*) is portrayed by a long violin solo. Strauss told Romain Rolland in 1900 that

it's my wife that I wanted to portray. She is very complex, very much a woman, a little perverse, something of a flirt, never twice alike, every minute different from what she was the minute before. At the beginning the Hero follows her, goes into the key in which she has just sung; but she always flies further away. Then, at the end, he says: 'No, I'm staying here'. He stays in his thoughts, in his own key. Then she comes to him.

It is but one of his many musical portraits of Pauline Strauss, culminating in the brilliant opera *Intermezzo* (1924).

But the swaggering, strong Hero of the opening section is certainly not Strauss, nor would he ever have seen himself in this light. 'I'm no hero,' he told Rolland, 'I haven't got the necessary strength; I'm not made for battle; I much prefer to go into retreat, to be peaceful and to rest. I haven't enough genius.' If one wishes to test the truth of this modest self-assessment, one has only to consider the facts of Strauss's apparent duping by the Nazis from 1933 to 1935 – the Hero of the start of *Ein Heldenleben* would never have allowed himself to become so compromised. Only a few years after composing *Heldenleben*, Strauss drew, without prevarication, his musical self-portrait in *Symphonia domestica*: as we shall see, the motifs are marked with such directions as 'easy-going', 'dreamy', 'morose'. Hardly the 'heroic strength' he required in the first section of *Ein Heldenleben*!

Willi Schuh, in the first volume of his biography of Strauss,[1] particularly cites the final section – 'the retirement from the world and self-fulfilment in contemplation' – as directly contrary to Strauss's attitude to life. Others have seen it as a forecast of his withdrawal, after 1908, into his villa at Garmisch, though it could scarcely be said that a man so busy ever 'retired from the world'. There is perhaps a deeper aspect to be considered here, though in a purely speculative sense. The impression of Strauss as a composer for whom emotion was only skin-deep, an impression fostered by Alma Mahler in particular, is a delusion. Of course Strauss fostered it too, and that is why we should be doubly suspicious. His desire for financial security and domestic comfort, his dislike of the winter months for composing, his card-playing, his compulsive need to compose even when inspiration came mechanically, and most of all his studied reticence about the inner substance of his music – might these not be clues to a compelling need to escape from some dark streak in his nature, some over-riding fear against which a sanguine temperament was the strongest but not necessarily the easiest weapon? And music provided the best of all escape-routes from such black nights of the soul, except that sometimes the fears surfaced in the music, in such lonely passages as Klytemnestra's nightmare aria in *Elektra*, in the Marschallin's final soliloquy in Act I of *Der Rosenkavalier* (what are such terrifyingly realistic truths doing in this ambience?), in several parts of *Die Frau ohne Schatten*, and, at the end, in *Metamorphosen* and the Oboe Concerto.

No composer as great and as accomplished as Strauss can be free from tensions in his creative nature. We can pinpoint the causes of those tensions in Strauss. They lie in his family life during his adolescence. His mother was highly strung to the point where she eventually required treatment in a mental hospital; his horn-playing father was embittered and short-tempered. The mother's illness depressed the father to the extent that Strauss had to act as mediator. Strauss tried to persuade his father that he had a duty to 'keep himself strong and fit by diverting and dispersing the dark thoughts'. That,

[1] *Richard Strauss: a Chronicle of the Early Years (1864–1898)*, translated by Mary Whittall (Cambridge, 1982).

surely, was also Strauss's aim in his music, and it also partly explains his refusal to be goaded by his temperamental wife's insults and disparagements. After all, he had seen it all before and what it could do. While not subscribing to the modish attribution of a 'death-wish' to most of the post-Wagnerian romantics, one may note the closing passages of *Tod und Verklärung, Don Quixote* and *Don Juan* and the *Four Last Songs* and ponder Strauss's vulnerability more deeply than has sometimes been the case. If he appeared to be all for a quiet life, it was because he knew the reverse side of the coin and was deeply pained and scared by it.

For *Ein Heldenleben* the Strauss orchestra was enlarged to include bass clarinet, double bassoon, eight horns, five trumpets, three trombones, tenor and bass tubas, elaborate percussion and a string section specified as no fewer than sixty-four players. In form it is a vast sonata movement, containing elements of a *scherzo* and *adagio*. There are six sections, none of them marked in the score: 1. The Hero. 2. The Hero's Adversaries (or critics). 3. The Hero's Companion (or wife). 4. The Hero's deeds of war. 5. The Hero's works of peace (and struggles in the face of continued criticism). 6. The Hero's retirement from the world and the fulfilment of his life.

Allowing that there will be some for whom this generous, passionate, large-gestured music will always be an embarrassment, others will regard it as one of the finest of orchestral showpieces and will enjoy its humour and wit, of which there is much, as well as its opulent outpouring of emotion. Part 1, the first-subject section, presents the Hero in a long dignified theme in E flat for horns and strings, pulsating with confidence and vigour, although the flattened notes in the seventh bar perhaps indicate feet of clay:

Ex.23

This theme spans nearly three octaves and truthfully conveys the impression of a powerful, not to say overbearing, personality. When it is restated new themes stem from it and the music is built to a succession of enormous climaxes, culminating in yet another grand restatement of Ex. 23. This is followed by a defiant challenge hurled out six times, each resulting in a brief, tense pause. Then the first bar of Ex. 23 is blasted from the brass section. A further pause ensues while the Hero waits to discover what he has stirred up by this militant display.

The answer is the Adversaries – the critics – depicted on woodwind, tubas and muted trombones as a spiteful, carping, grumbling bunch. Strauss has been rebuked for this section on the grounds that he had not, on the whole, been badly treated by critics. This is only partially true. He had had his share of unintelligent verdicts passed on his work. In any case, this is not a bad-tempered section and one should give Strauss credit for having some fun at the critics' expense. But there is no doubt that their barbs upset the Hero, whose principal theme (Ex. 23) goes into the minor on cellos and basses. These instruments also play a new and doleful melody incorporating the last two bars of Ex. 23. It increases in fervour and then dies away, enabling the critics to return with renewed venom to the offensive. But the Hero is no longer downcast; he retaliates with salvoes from the brass.

Now appears the reason for his new-found courage: his *Gefährtin*, impersonated by the violin in one of the longest and most difficult solo passages allotted to the orchestral leader. She has three principal themes, each of a loving nature, but they are interspersed with brilliant cadenzas including arpeggios, glissandi, double and treble stoppings and rapid scale passages. Lavish instructions in the score betray its importance to Strauss. Here are some of them: 'languishing; frivolous; tender; somewhat sentimental; very brisk and vivacious; very sharp; lazily; very calm; playful; lovable; merry; very feelingly; urgent and vehement; angry; shrewish; tender and loving'. The Companion's charm and capriciousness arouse the Hero: a rising fourth is common to all his replies to her. Hesitant at first, he becomes frankly amorous and launches into a passionate love scene, decked out with harp glissandi, garlands of trills on woodwind, erotic horns and caressing strings. It is one of Strauss's most gorgeous love scenes and has this tender afterglow (Ex. 24 opposite). But even in this bliss the Hero's mind is still on the critics, whose

Ex. 24

nattering is heard in the background. His Companion's hand soothes his brow with a gentle reminder of Ex. 24. When a call to action is sounded by three off-stage trumpets, the Hero cannot be restrained and Ex. 23 is egged on by the Companion's principal theme as he prepares for battle.

This fourth section, the Battle Scene as it is generally called, aroused violent reactions when it was new. Today, our ears accustomed not only to the sound of real battles but to much more discordant use of the orchestra, it still sounds strident and exhilarating, but its structure is easily perceived and we know that it is far removed from being the 'musical chaos' it was once thought to be. When Rolland attended an early Berlin performance he said he 'saw people shudder . . ., suddenly rise to their feet and make violent and unconscious gestures'. The English critic Arthur Johnstone, a generally sympathetic and percipient Straussian, wrote in the *Manchester Guardian* in 1904 that the Battle Scene 'is not music, and does nothing whatever for music. It is a monstrous excrescence and blemish – a product of musical insanity, bearing no trace whatever of that genius which produced the lovely and perfect *Tod und Verklärung* . . .' Strong stuff.

Opinions and tastes move on. The Battle Scene is a symphonic development section, too novel for its day but no longer difficult to follow. An aggressive rhythm is battered out on the percussion. Over it, in the brass, is a new version of one of the Adversaries' themes. The first four bars of Ex. 23 enlist for the Hero, with the trumpet-call appended. As the din intensifies, the Companion's theme is heard – inspiration for the Hero – and the Hero's main theme (Ex. 23) gradually returns at fuller length with its subsidiaries from Section 1. The Adversaries counterattack persistently, but the Hero wins and at the moment of triumph it is the love themes that are exultantly proclaimed. Ex. 23 becomes a victory hymn and is then combined with the Companion's principal theme. It sounds as if a conventional recapitulation has begun, but after six bars a new and thrusting melody surges from the strings, oboes and trumpets (Ex. 25 overleaf).

Ex.25

The effect of this superb new invention is to refocus the inventive spirit of the whole work. Strauss uses it as the generative force of a gigantic climax at the height of which he brings off a remarkable *coup de théâtre* when the horns let fly with the great theme from *Don Juan* (Ex. 11, p. 20). This is followed on strings and woodwind by the love theme from the same work (Ex. 8, p. 19), and the Spirit of Man theme from *Also sprach Zarathustra* (Ex. 16, p. 32). An expectant pause is ended by the two tubas who pontificate in the voice of the critic who took no part in the battle. The Hero lashes back but calms down in preparation for the fifth section, the Works of Peace, a recapitulatory reverie in which Strauss summarises his music up to this point. It begins with the start of Ex. 23 in a new rhythm, with one of its subsidiaries played in canon by cor anglais and bassoon. One by one, fragments of themes from Strauss works are heard, skilfully woven into a seamless texture. There are thirty-one quotations from nine works. Here, for the listener's interest, is a list (score references are to the Edition Eulenburg miniature score, No. 498. The bar indicated is that in which the quotation begins; some quotations are several bars in length, others only a brief allusion in one bar):

1. *Don Juan* (p. 165, five bars after fig. 83, horns).
2. *Don Juan* (p. 165, seven bars after 83, violins and woodwind).
3. *Also sprach Zarathustra* (p. 165, seven bars after 83, cellos, bass clarinet, four horns).
4. *Tod und Verklärung* (p. 172, fig. 87, cellos and double basses, the *Idealism* theme, Ex. 12).
5. *Tod und Verklärung* (p. 172, fig. 87, violins, 'childhood' theme).
6. *Don Quixote* (p. 173, three bars after fig. 87, flutes, 'knightly' theme, Ex. 19).
7. *Don Quixote* (p. 173, four bars after fig. 87, cor anglais).
8. *Don Quixote* (p. 173, five bars after fig. 87, strings, 'courtesy' theme, Ex. 20).
9. *Don Juan* (p. 174, fig. 88, oboe, love theme, Ex. 10).
10. *Don Juan* (p. 174, fig. 88, violas and cellos, wooing theme, Ex. 9).
11. *Don Quixote* (p. 174, fig. 88, bass clarinet, 'shepherd' theme).
12. *Till Eulenspiegel* (p. 174, three bars after fig. 88, clarinet and bass clarinet, 'rascal' theme, Ex. 14).
13. *Guntram* (p. 175, six bars after fig. 88, clarinet, love theme, Act I).

14. *Guntram* (p. 176, fig. 89, violins, 'Freihild' theme, Act I).
15. *Guntram* (p. 176, two bars after fig. 89, trombone, 'Freihild's future' theme, Act III).
16. *Guntram* (p. 177, sixth bar after fig. 89, fifth horn, 'Guntram' theme, Prelude, Act I).
17. *Tod und Verklärung* (p. 177, seventh bar after fig. 89, tenor tuba, *Idealism* theme, Ex. 12).
18. *Also sprach Zarathustra* (p. 177, seventh bar after fig. 89, trumpets, 'Nature'-motif). This is combined with
19. *Guntram* (p. 177, seventh bar after fig. 89, trumpets, love duet, Act III).
20. *Macbeth* (p. 178, fig. 90, cellos, basses, bass clarinet, bassoon, double bassoon, 'Lady Macbeth' theme, Ex. 3).
21. *Befreit* (song, bars 20–22) (p. 178, one bar after fig. 90, oboes and first violins).
22. *Macbeth* (p. 178, two bars after fig. 90, violas, one of principal 'Macbeth' themes, Ex. 2).
23. *Macbeth* (p. 178, three bars after fig. 90, cor anglais, 'Kingship' theme, Ex. 1).
24. *Traum durch die Dämmerung* (song, bars 15–18) (p. 179, six bars after fig. 89, violas, tenor tuba, bass clarinet).
25. *Guntram* (p. 179, seven bars after fig. 89, E flat clarinet, 'Duke's' theme, Act II).
26. *Guntram* (p. 180, fig. 91, violins, Prelude, Act I).
27. *Don Quixote* (p. 180, fig. 91, cor anglais, horns, cellos, 'Knight errantry' theme in Var. 3).
28. *Guntram* (p. 181, six bars after 91, third and fourth horns, 'Guntram' theme from Prelude, Act I).
29. *Tod und Verklärung* (p. 182, fig. 92, cellos, *appassionato* theme).
30. *Also sprach Zarathustra* (p. 182, three bars after fig. 92, clarinets, horns, trumpets, 'Spirit of Man' theme).
31. *Guntram* (p. 183, four bars after fig. 92, trombones, brief motif from Prelude, Act I).

Interwoven into this gorgeous tapestry are the various themes of the Hero and his Companion. When the quotations are completed, an impassioned version of the challenging theme from the first section is twice played by high woodwind. Back comes the ponderous reply from the two-tubas critic. In a frenzy of self-doubt, the Hero fills the air with turbulent cries and savage dissonances derived from his principal themes. The struggle subsides into a chord of C major. It is time for the coda.

Over a steady but irregular drum rhythm, the cor anglais plays a bucolic melody based on Ex. 23. This passage is designedly similar to that in which Don Quixote returns home from his adventures. The music wends its way back to the tonic of E flat; strings and the full complement of eight horns play the serene, noble melody which symbolises the Hero's contentment. This is a derivant of the theme with which he lashed back at the critic after the battle, and that, in its turn, was derived from one of the Companion's loving themes. In such ways is *Ein Heldenleben* given its structural and emotional unity. The Hero's world seems now to be peaceful, but suddenly a nightmare recurs: the Adversaries' first theme, with snarling brass. But the Companion (violin solo) is at hand to comfort him. Contentment is restored and the glowing Ex. 24 returns on the horn, combining and alternating with two of the tender love themes. Gently the solo violin ascends and the horn descends to their respective E flat while the brass swell out an E flat chord from the very opening of Ex. 23.

This was not how *Ein Heldenleben* originally ended. Strauss completed the score in Berlin on 1 December 1898, when the work ended *pianissimo* with the solo horn and solo violin. His biographer Willi Schuh has revealed that Strauss's friend Friedrich Rösch jocularly said, 'Richard, that's another *pianissimo* close. The public simply won't believe you can end *forte*!!'[1] On 23 December, an entry in Strauss's diary states: 'Began to score the new ending of *Heldenleben*.' He completed it four days later. He had added the sequence of rising chords for woodwind and brass which begin *piano* on the trumpet, rise from *mezzo forte* to *fortissimo* and fade to *mezzo forte*, with the final chord *piano, molto diminuendo*. Schuh tells a delightful story of the 82-year-old Strauss listening to a rehearsal in Zürich in 1946, winking at him during the final bars and whispering: 'State funeral!' But it is the state funeral of an opera conductor and composer, not of the Kaiser's laureate nor of Nietzsche's Superman, nor of Rolland's Nero.

Symphonia Domestica[2] *(Domestic Symphony), Op. 53*

Strauss conducted the first performance of *Ein Heldenleben* in Frankfurt on 3 March 1899. Berlin first heard it nineteen days later. It was to be the last première of a Strauss tone poem for five years. Significantly, the next two works in the series had the word 'symphony' in their titles. With *Heldenleben* out of the way, Strauss began in the spring of 1899 to write a libretto for an opera to be called *Ekke und Schnittlein*. This was abandoned. He returned to the idea of a

[1] *Chronicle of the Early Years*, op. cit.

[2] Strauss, a classicist, would surely resent the frequent conversion of his Latin title into the Italian *Sinfonia domestica*.

'Spring Symphony' but made no progress; he began, in 1900, to compose music for *Die Künstlertragödie (The Artist's Tragedy)* and he wrote the scenario of a ballet, *Kythere*, and composed a fair amount of music for it from which he quarried themes for several of his later works. The years 1899 to 1901 were a prolific period for Strauss lieder, but his principal preoccupation was with the one-act opera, or *Singgedicht, Feuersnot*. The libretto was written by Ernst von Wolzogen and the idea of the work was, as Strauss confessed, 'to wreak some vengeance on my dear native town [Munich] where I . . . just like the great Richard [Wagner] thirty years before, had had such unpleasant experiences'. Although Strauss exaggerated the conservatism of Munich, he felt it had never given him sufficient recognition and he was irked by the opera Intendant's persistent opposition to his demands. When the Berlin Court Opera offered him a ten-year contract from 1 November 1898, he eagerly accepted. He conducted his last Munich opera performance on 18 October – it was *Fidelio*. Then 'off and away – into your arms!' he wrote to Pauline.

Feuersnot, which the taste of the day judged slightly indecent, had its first performance on 21 November 1901, in Dresden. In Berlin the Empress was so shocked she ordered its removal from the repertoire after the seventh performance. But at any rate Strauss had ended the opera jinx which had unsettled him since *Guntram*. (His statement that after the failure of *Guntram* he 'lost the courage' to compose operas needs to be regarded with scepticism in view of the number of operatic projects which he contemplated. He was awaiting the right libretto.) In May 1902 he began the short score of a new orchestral work. This was completed in July 1903 and fully scored by 31 December. It was to be called *Symphonia domestica* and this time there was no attempt to deny that the domesticity was Strauss's own – the work represents twenty-four hours in the Strauss household. (British readers may like to know that he worked on the closing stages of the composition sketch while on holiday in the Isle of Wight after the Strauss Festival in London in 1903.)

The *Symphonia domestica* has been the butt of much insensitive and inept criticism and Strauss probably came to regret his disclosures that the music described the baby being bathed, the parents quarrelling and making love, and the relatives remarking on how like Papa or Mama the baby was. The first shots of misunderstanding were fired before the work was finished, when Strauss's old father objected that the word 'domestic' implied servitude and would 'place the whole centre of gravity on the matter of inferiority'. The bathing of the baby drew an uncharacteristic joke from Hans Richter in which he said that the destruction of Valhalla had not made a quarter the noise of a Bavarian baby in its bath – a palpable exaggeration even if a delightful remark, and at least it was good-natured. Ernest Newman thought the orchestral colour 'overdone', the polyphony 'often coarse and sprawling', and the realistic effects 'so pitiably foolish that one listens to them with regret that a composer of genius should ever have fallen so low'.

Romain Rolland, though he acknowledged the stature of the music, found the erotic love scene 'in extremely bad taste', and it is no surprise to find Norman Del Mar agreeing with him and describing this episode as 'somehow disagreeable' and the programme 'intolerable'. Barbara Tuchman, of course, is left with a 'dominant impression' of 'thumping and screaming and raucous confusion suggesting a maddened circus'. She adds gratuitously and incomprehensibly: 'If this is German home life, German history becomes understandable.' The American music critic Lawrence Gilman wrote, at the time of the work's first performance in New York, that 'only a Teuton with a Teuton's failure of tact' could have composed *Domestica*, which proves that it was scarcely the music that was under review. It is astonishing, too, that some critics today are as incapable as their predecessors of eighty years ago of perceiving humour and irony in Strauss and, even more culpably, of appreciating the music for its own sake. For although, as in *Don Quixote*, the programme is most graphically illustrated, it is superfluous to a full enjoyment of what Herbert von Karajan has bravely and rightly described as 'one of Strauss's finest works'. Strauss himself, in a letter about *Domestica* written to Rolland on 5 July 1905, summed up once and for all his 'philosophy' about programme-music:

For me the poetic programme is nothing more than the initial cause which shapes the forms in which I then give expression and purely musical development to my feelings; not, as you suppose, merely a *musical description* of certain events in real life. That, after all, would be completely contrary to the spirit of music. But if the music is not to seep away in pure wilfulness, it needs certain boundaries to define the form, and a programme serves as a canal-bank. Even for the listener an analytical programme of that kind should be no more than a guide. Whoever is interested should use it. Whoever really understands how to listen to music probably has no need of it.

Point is given to Richter's joke by the size of the orchestra for which the *Symphonia domestica* is written – nearly 110 players, including five clarinets, four (optional) saxophones, and sixty-two strings. But, like Mahler, Strauss often uses this huge array as if it were an octet. Another comparison with Mahler suggests itself: the *Domestica* is the Straussian equivalent of the Fourth Symphony in its tenderness, conscious naïveté and relaxed rapture. (Mahler, incidentally, conducted the first Vienna performance.) The symphonic structure is quasi-Mahlerian, too, in that the work divides into two parts although the four movements of a classical symphony are discernible. Part 1 comprises an introduction, *scherzo* and *adagio*, while Part 2 is the fugal finale and epilogue. Yet the one continuous movement form of the tone poem is paramount. Many sensible commentators have been troubled (as Richter obviously was) by the disparity between the intimacy of the subject-matter and the size of the forces used to express it. There is some substance in this criticism but no more than may be applied to nearly all late-romantic music. Strauss's use of a large orchestra was his natural mode of expression and undoubtedly there is an operatic projection of the subject-matter in this work. But the lightness of texture and the song-like nature of several passages are entirely appropriate.

It is apparent from the light-fingered opening, with its succession of short motifs, that Strauss has reverted to the fantastic manner of *Don Quixote*. Gone is the sonorous, long-paragraphed style appropriate to the heroic life. Here is Don Riccardo ready to venture forth on his adventures in his Charlottenburg residence. Strauss depicts himself in a succession of moods, each characterised by specific instruments: easy-going (cellos), dreamy (oboe), morose (clarinet), fiery (strings) and merry (trumpets). The most significant of these is the first, played by the cellos:

Ex.26

Bewegt gemächlich
Cellos

Pauline's motifs follow: tender, hot-tempered and waspish. The first three notes of her first theme, for flute, oboe and violins, are the direct inversion of her husband's (Ex. 27 overleaf). The Husband and Wife groups of themes are combined and alternated in a contrapuntal display comparable in expertise with the complemen-

Ex.27

sehr lebhaft
Flute, Oboe, Violins

tary passage in *Don Quixote*.

It is then time for the Child to complete the family portrait. He does so through the unusual medium of the oboe d'amore, accompanied by tremolando chords on the second violins. His theme is really the work's principal subject:

Ex.28

ruhig   sehr zart
Ob. d'am.

The Child's lung-power is soon demonstrated with trills on woodwind and muted trumpets, and (at fig. 18 in the score) we then come to the famous passage where two muted trumpets marked *Die Tanten* (*The Aunts*) say 'Ganz der Papa!' ('How like his father!') and *Die Onkels* (*The Uncles*) on muted trombone retort 'Ganz die Mama!'

For the start of the *scherzo* the Child's theme becomes a lilting folk-like melody. The delicacy of scoring and lightness of touch in this section are wholly delightful and Strauss's craftsmanship is nowhere more admirable than at the climax, where the *scherzando* section of the Child's theme (oboe, clarinets and bassoons) is combined with its original form (oboe d'amore, cor anglais, horns, violins and violas). A new and tender theme, of wide melodic range and anticipating one in the opera *Capriccio* of forty years later, merges with versions of the parents' theme as the trio section, the famous bath, approaches. This is merely a return of the wind and brass trills heard earlier, and comes from the same seam of invention as the sheep in *Don Quixote*. When it subsides, Strauss bases a lullaby on the Venetian Gondolier's Song from Mendelssohn's *Lieder ohne Worte*, orchestrates it like the Marschallin's soliloquy on the passage of time in Act I of *Der Rosenkavalier* and, as the clock (glockenspiel) strikes 7 pm, writes a serenely beautiful reverie for flute, oboe, clarinet and bass clarinet, a meditation on the Husband's second (dreamy) motif. A brief irruption of the Wife's first theme (Ex. 27) leads into the *adagio* section.

The first part of this slow-movement section is constructed from the Husband's themes, with references to the Wife's. It is the work's development and its beginning is said to represent Strauss in his study. Inspiration seizes him with a majestically rich version for strings of his second motif. The return of the Wife's Ex. 27 in an augmentation on the basses is the signal for the start of the Love Scene, which builds to a passionate and erotic climax of such graphic detail that it makes the *Rosenkavalier* Act I prelude's depiction of the sexual act seem relatively tame. This conjugal union is followed by a coda in which the couple's dreams are suggested in music of impressionistically visionary and imaginative harmonic quality (they include memories of the Child's bath).

The striking of 7 am begins the finale – 'Double fugue, lusty arguments – reconciliation – happy ending'. The household wakens noisily. The *scherzo* section of the Child's theme becomes the first subject of the fugue, the second being a compendium of the Wife's motifs. The Husband's themes are also introduced and the working-out of the fugue – the lusty argument – is a passage of brilliant orchestration and even more brilliant thematic manipulation. Soon it is the Child's theme (on violins) which predominates and guides the music towards an exquisite and again folk-like episode for flutes, oboe d'amore, cor anglais, clarinet, bass clarinet, bassoons and horns. After this, the symphony goes exuberantly to its virtuosic end with joyful versions of all the principal themes, the Child's especially. Horns are taken up to high A and a triple *forte* reiteration of the first notes of Ex. 26 gives the Husband the last word.

Symphonia domestica, as Strauss himself said, must be played exceedingly well and accurately. Its difficulties are one factor in its relative neglect (it is, of course, expensive to perform, too). Another has undoubtedly been the curious notion that a symphony about home life is somehow not to be taken seriously. 'What can be more serious a matter than married life?' Strauss asked. 'Marriage is the most serious happening in life, and the holy joy over such a union is intensified by the arrival of a child. Yet life has naturally got its funny side, and this I have also introduced into the work in order to enliven it. But I want the symphony to be taken seriously . . .' Exactly the same public (or critical) attitude for years kept Strauss's *opera domestica, Intermezzo*, in the nether regions of the repertoire. Its comedy was overstressed and it has been mainly to the credit of Glyndebourne that the work's essential seriousness and musical strengths have been at last revealed without any loss of amusement.

The opinion that *Symphonia domestica* initiated a decline is no longer seriously tenable. It is one of the best composed of all Strauss's works, superior in this respect to *Ein Heldenleben*, which is episodic by comparison, and not far short of *Don Quixote*. The organic unity of the music is secured by the most concentrated and intricate variants of the principal motifs. The scoring is splendidly accomplished, even the grandiose passages making their effect without blatancy, and the contrapuntal skill is of a high order. The thematic invention is consistently fresh and inspired. To say that it is familiar in its outlines is only to say that it is entirely characteristic of its creator. In the spontaneous combustion of the *Domestica* themes we descry the beginnings of the marvellous imaginative flights of *Salome*. More than in any of its predecessors, we can find in *Domestica* the Strauss of the operas. It is but a short step to the vivid characterisations of *Salome, Elektra* and *Der Rosenkavalier*, and its self-portraiture, more accurate than in *Ein Heldenleben*, is a forerunner of the operatic self-portraits of Barak, Morosus and Storch. 'Chevalley [Hermann Chevalley, the Hamburg music critic] advises me against always composing myself,' Strauss wrote in 1905. 'Do you know a composer who has ever composed anything but himself? Funny people these aestheticians!' The *Symphonia domestica* is central to any appreciation of Strauss the musician that goes beyond superficial appraisal of his most obvious skills.

Eine Alpensinfonie (An Alpine Symphony), Op. 64

The last, largest and longest in the great line of Strauss tone poems had been lurking in the composer's mind for many years. From childhood he had loved the mountains and the sights and sounds of nature, and in his early manhood he planned a symphonic triptych about Nature of which an Alpine symphony would form part. In 1900, as already stated, he sketched some music for an opera, *Die Künstlertragödie*: it began with a sunrise. The theme found its way into the *Alpensinfonie*. But it was not until 1911 that sketches for the symphony began to take shape. Having completed *Der Rosenkavalier* and supervised its successful launching, Strauss was fidgety for more operatic work. Hofmannsthal had tantalised him with the idea of *Die*

EINE ALPENSINFONIE

Frau ohne Schatten and Strauss was anxious to get down to it — 'meanwhile', he wrote to his librettist, 'I worry myself with a symphony, which is giving me less enjoyment than shaking cockchafers from a tree'. He was soon diverted into the opera *Ariadne auf Naxos* and to the ballet *Josephslegende*. In 1913 he produced two works which are in some ways closely related to the *Alpensinfonie*, first through the use of vast orchestral forces, secondly through contrapuntal mastery. The first was the *Festliches Präludium*, an occasional piece composed for the opening of the Vienna Konzerthaus, the second the magnificent Rückert setting, *Deutsche Motette*, a masterpiece of *a cappella* writing for four soloists and 16-part mixed chorus. The *Motette* is a major Strauss work, yet it receives only scanty consideration in so wide-ranging a study as Norman Del Mar's three volumes. During 1914 and 1915 he began to compose *Die Frau ohne Schatten* and completed the *Alpensinfonie* on 8 February 1915, having orchestrated it in a hundred days from 1 November 1914. The idea, once persistently propagated, of Strauss 'composing by memory' after *Rosenkavalier* is now so laughable that one can only assume that its perpetrators did not know, or even want to know, the subsequent works.

Strauss had intended to dedicate the *Alpensinfonie* to Ernst von Schuch, conductor of the Dresden Court Opera, where four of his operas had had outstanding first performances, but Schuch died in May 1914. So the score bears the inscription 'Dedicated in gratitude to Count Nicolaus Seebach and the Royal Orchestra, Dresden' (Seebach had been Intendant of the Dresden Court Opera since 1894), and it was this orchestra which gave the first performance on 28 October 1915, when Strauss conducted it in Berlin.

The orchestra is swollen to 150 players, mainly by the off-stage brass section of twelve horns, two trumpets and two trombones used in the Ascent section when a distant hunting party is heard, and by the percussion required for the storm and other special effects (wind machine, thunder machine, glockenspiel, cymbals, triangle, cowbells, tam-tam and various drums). A Heckelphone, E flat clarinet and four tenor tubas are also called upon for preciseness of tone-colour. Otherwise the basic orchestra is four each of woodwind and brass, two harps, organ and a full complement of strings. This indulgence in opulent forces is not a manifestation of that megalomania on which Strauss's critics insist and which will, I hope, by now be regarded by the reader as illusory. Strauss was a child of his time, and he used the full resources of the post-Wagnerian symphony orchestra as his birthright, as did Elgar, Mahler, Schoenberg, Stravinsky and Ravel. In Berlin and Dresden he was accustomed to having an orchestra of almost this size at his daily disposal.

'I wanted for once to compose just as a cow gives milk,' Strauss said of the *Alpensinfonie*. After a rehearsal he remarked: 'Now at last I have learned to orchestrate.' To Hofmannsthal, on 15 November 1915, he wrote: 'You must hear the *Alpensinfonie* . . . it is really a fine work!' And when he returned to London in 1947 after the Second World War, he wanted to conduct the *Alpine*, although various difficulties necessitated eventual substitution of the *Symphonia domestica*. So it may be deduced that he had a particular affection for this much-maligned work, as other composers have had for works of theirs which had failed to win the hoped-for admiration.

The 'cow giving milk' simile backfired on Strauss. A cow gives milk in an entirely uncritical way; the liquid just pours forth. Was this not exactly what was wrong with the *Alpensinfonie*? With such a remark Strauss delivered himself into the hands of those who find in the easy-going (and easy-listening) pictorialism of the work a lack of moral substance and a feebleness of artistic resolve. Such critics wanted Strauss to be a different composer from the one he was. (Hofmannsthal was always taunting him with ignoring intellectual standards.) One does not go to Strauss for Bruckner's spiritual fervour, Beethoven's intellectual power and Mahler's humanitarian misgivings and doubts. There is depth in Strauss's music, as any listener to *Don Quixote* can discover, but he is primarily entertainer and observer rather than moral philosopher. None of his operas is a tragedy, though tragic and serious events occur in them. Presumably a cow enjoys giving milk, and in every bar of the *Alpensinfonie* one can sense Strauss enjoying composing this tribute to the panorama of the Zugspitze and the Wettersteingebirge which he saw from his Garmisch home. The responsive listener, untroubled by intellectual mountaineering, can enjoy it too, while acknowledging that it is not, as a composition, on the consistently inspired level of *Don Quixote*. The themes are not all out of Strauss's top drawer – recapitulation rather than exposition – but they are striking in their memorability and in the way they lend themselves to the wondrous colours in which Strauss decks them. An understanding interpreter will uncover the solemnity of the music's nature-worship, its awareness of an elemental power, which raises it far above the level of mere travelogue to which those in severest antipathy to it would reduce it; at the same time, the listener who seeks the pantheistic and mystical lure of the mountains must go to Delius's *Song of the High Hills*. In the end what counts is if a worthwhile musical experience is had by the listener to *Eine Alpensinfonie*, and there can be no reasonable doubt of that. One does not listen to it with the same pair of ears one reserves for Stravinsky's *Perséphone*, nor, for that matter, for Strauss's *Le bourgeois gentilhomme*.

The work is divided into twenty-two continuous sections, which are marked in the score. They are:

Nacht (Night); Sonnenaufgang (Sunrise); Der Anstieg (The Ascent); Eintritt in den Wald (Entry into the Forest); Wanderung neben dem Bache (Wandering by the Stream); Am Wasserfall (By the Waterfall); Erscheinung (Apparition); Auf blumige Wiesen (On the flowering meadows); Auf der Alm (On the pastures); Durch Dickicht und Gestrüpp auf Irrwegen (Through thicket and brier to wrong paths); Auf dem Gletscher (On the glacier); Gefahrevolle Augenblicke (Dangerous moments); Auf dem Gipfel (On the Summit); Vision (Vision); Nebel steigen auf (Mists arise); Die Sonne verdüstert sich allmählich (The Sun gradually darkens); Elegie (Elegy); Stille vor dem Sturm (Calm before the storm); Gewitter und Sturm, Abstieg (Thunderstorm, Descent); Sonnenuntergang (Sunset); Ausklang (Echo); Nacht (Night).

Detailed description of the music is hardly necessary after such a synopsis, but certain features need to be identified. How far is the 'symphony' of the title justified? Less than in *Domestica*, but the listener will recognise a *scherzo* and an *andante* in addition to a striding *allegro*. But if structurally Strauss was stretching the term, there is no denying the symphonic 'feel' of the work. It is composed with such apparently effortless mastery that the twenty-two sections soon become an irrelevance and one is swept along by the music's grandeur and colour.

As for the scoring, it is beyond comparison, even by Strauss's own standards, in its richness and splendour, but even more memorably in the economy of many of the most striking passages, in the subtle and variegated effects obtained by extensive division of the strings, and in the linear clarity of some of the most intimate episodes. Some writers have expressed surprise that the 'mammoth' *Alpensinfonie* should have lain on Strauss's desk alongside the 37-instrument score of *Ariadne auf Naxos*. But have they listened carefully to the *Eintritt in den Wald*, where the scoring is in the *Ariadne* vein (and the melodic invention a reminiscence of a Marschallin monologue!)? Then there is the opening, that magnificent picture of a mountain shrouded in night. The strings have a unison B flat. A descending scale has each note sustained until every degree is heard at the same time. Trombones and tuba play the mountain's theme in chords (it is the work's principal *leitmotiv*):

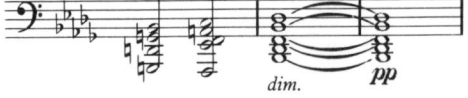

Ex.29

It changes key from B flat minor to D minor, giving rise to an example of Straussian polytonality as the new key is opposed by the sustained notes of the B flat minor scale on the strings. After this tenebrous introduction, the texture becomes animated over a long tonic pedal held by the woodwind – Strauss was so worried about the strain he was putting on the players' breath-control here that he recommended a device (now obsolete) called a 'Samuel's Aerophor'[1] which supplied oxygen to the performer through a tube worked by a foot-pump.

The sun rises to a majestic transformation of the descending scale which opened the symphony, followed by a new theme for the horns. A purposeful march-theme beginning on the lower strings signals the start of the Ascent (Ex. 30 opposite). An ecstatic fanfare for horns, trumpets and trombones may be taken as expressive of the climbers' awe of the peak they are to climb. They hear a distant hunting party before they move into wooded country. Forest murmurings on the strings accompany a new melody for horns and trombones. In the *Ariadne*-like development section, Ex. 30 is given to the strings, with woodwind decorations, and for a few bars Strauss veers between a string quartet and the full strings in some of the most characteristic contrapuntal invention in the symphony. The pastoral mood is continued in the three subsequent sections. Strauss revels in the cascades of tone he elicits from each part of the orchestra to depict the waterfall, and he rivals Tchaikovsky (in *Manfred*) in the delicacy of the theme for oboes by which he summons up the apparition of the

[1] Strauss mis-spelt this as 'Aerophon' in the autograph.

EINE ALPENSINFONIE

Ex.30

Alpine Sprite who lives in the rainbow created by the spray. Strauss glides out of this section and into the pleasant verdure of the flowering meadows by means of an expressively simple new melody for horns and violas (successively a descending third, fourth and fifth):

Ex.31

Ex. 30 on the cellos is the groundswell over which woodwind, harps and pizzicato violas suggest the picturesque scene. This bucolic movement ends on the *Alm*, a pasture where cattle are put to graze during the Alpine summer. Mahlerian cowbells, birdsong and yodelling coalesce to provide an idyll.

Woodwind shriek a danger warning which the horns' reassurance does nothing to negate as the music becomes intensely chromatic when the climbers encounter rough going and lose their way – as Strauss did in the Alps when he was a boy. Arrival on the glacier brings ecstatic declarations of the chief *leitmotiv* (Ex. 29) by the full orchestra, but before the summit is reached jagged notes on muted trumpets and an agitated chromatic pizzicato signify dangerous moments. Ex. 30 returns on a solo cello accompanied by tremolandi on the violins and brilliant fragmented writing for trumpet and clarinets in preparation for the conquest of the summit, announced by the trombones:

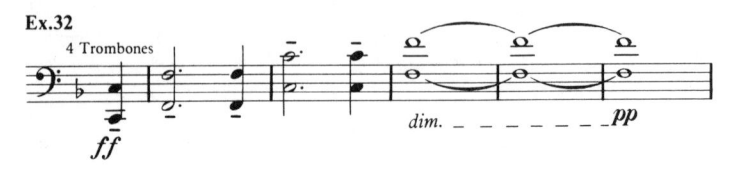

Ex.32

An oboe echoes hesitantly through the stillness, and then Strauss creates the sumptuous polyphonic climax one has been awaiting as several of the principal melodies are combined – Exx. 32, 29, 31 and the sunrise motif. (One cannot forbear to quote Hugo Cole's witticism that after all their efforts, the climbers' reward is only a popular theme from Bruch's G minor Violin Concerto (Ex. 31). Enjoyment of this observation is not diminished even if one counters that part of Strauss's genius lay in making Alpine mountains out of lesser men's foothills.)

The work's most extraordinary passage – *Vision* – follows. It is a development section in F sharp, eerie and abounding in trills, harp *arpeggiandos* and chromatic sequences for woodwind and based on Exx. 31 and 32, with Ex. 29 returning on the brass in the original key of B flat minor. When the sunrise theme returns, the organ makes its first entry, contributing to the ominous and oppressive atmosphere as the sun is obscured by mist. The strings are muted in the curious *Elegie* which precedes the drum-rolls, staccato D flats on the oboe, wails on the clarinet, and cracks of thunder which herald the outbreak of the storm – a passage, though overlong, in which Strauss stages a staggering display of art imitating nature. It is merged with the Descent, the work's recapitulation. The waterfall, the glacier, the moments of danger, the pastoral slopes are all revisited as the storm renews its violence. But with a final thunderclap and the last heavy raindrops, the clouds clear and the mountain is again sunlit (brass and organ, with strings soaring as Strauss alone could make them).

So the coda is reached – sunset is a brass chorale, the organ part is prominent, and for the *Ausklang* (*Echo*) Strauss moves into E flat, with the horns instructed to play 'in soft ecstasy'. Some of the most beautiful parts of the score are recalled and irradiated afresh. The writing for the strings is of a sustained tenderness and intensity rare even in Strauss. We are back in a sombre B flat minor and the symphony ends as it began, with night enfolding the mountain. Last rays from the sun gleam here and there – on violins, on brass – but at the end all light is extinguished, to complete this epitaph to a musical epoch which virtually ended in the years while it was being composed. Perhaps that was one reason why Strauss chose to make his largest orchestral work one from which the human factor, tragic, humorous, fantastic or erotic, is absent. 'Worship of nature, eternal and magnificent', Strauss's words about this symphony, were the nearest he ever came, or ever would have come, to a religious declaration. It is also possibly one explanation why he associated the work with the Antichrist.

Aftermath

Disappointment persists, among those who believe that Strauss turned his face away from any further harmonic 'adventures' after *Elektra*, that the Alpine ascent was made to such comfortable and euphonious sounds. Strauss knew what kind of music each situation demanded from him, and he had shown in *Elektra* that he could rival anybody in composing neurasthenic hysteria (even though a close study of that fascinating score reveals that it is not as 'advanced' as is sometimes claimed – Strauss knew how to make it sound advanced). Before a less prejudiced perspective on Strauss's completed life's work began to emerge, it was axiomatic to believe that the reason the tone poems grew longer was that Strauss had less to say and resorted to magniloquent note-spinning. I believe there were sounder reasons for their enlargement in span and scope. One was that, after 1895, Strauss was beginning to think instinctively on an operatic scale. The other was that, more than has yet been acknowledged or than the two men themselves might have admitted, there was considerable mutual influence between Strauss and Mahler.

Strauss's influence on Mahler has received some critical attention, but less has been paid to the reverse process. They were the outstanding conductor-composers of their day, dominating operatic and concert-hall life in Germany, Austria and Holland at the end of the nineteenth century from their successive bases in Hamburg, Vienna, Weimar, Munich and Berlin. From about 1895 they regularly conducted each other's works. Strauss in Berlin arranged for Mahler to conduct his Second Symphony there. Mahler conducted Strauss's operas in Vienna and the tone poems as they appeared. Though Strauss in later years affected to dismiss Mahler's compositions, there is no doubt that he had admired and learned from them. He saw on what scale Mahler could cope with programmatic symphonies and it is no coincidence that, from *Don Quixote* onwards, a Mahlerian symphonic mode of thought governs the tone poems, taking over from the more compact Lisztian models of the 1880s and early 1890s. Strauss's last Lisztian tone poem was *Also sprach Zarathustra*.

Strauss was sketching *Eine Alpensinfonie* in May 1911 when news of Mahler's death reached him. It affected him deeply; he said so to Hofmannsthal. The strange, almost spiritual atmosphere which haunts the works and which stays in the mind longer than its graphic descriptions, amazing though they are, may justly be regarded as Strauss's tribute to his great colleague, who would surely have admired the absolute orchestral mastery displayed in every bar, a mastery that was hard won, for by what right do we assume that Strauss did not experience the 'agonies' of creation merely because he made light of them?

If *Eine Alpensinfonie* was Strauss's farewell to Mahler, it was also his farewell to the tone poem, though not to orchestral works. It would be remiss not to mention the symphonic interlude between Scenes 3 and 4 of Act II of *Intermezzo*, where Strauss illustrates Storch's (i.e. his own) conducting activities with a miniature Strauss tone poem which manages cunningly to suggest features of the famous series without directly quoting from any. It is more than self-parody. The nearest he came in his old age to a tone poem in the style of his youth was in 1940, when he accepted a commission for a composition to celebrate the (spurious) 2600th anniversary of the Japanese imperial dynasty. (Several composers were approached for works, including Benjamin Britten, whose *Sinfonia da Requiem* was rejected because of its Christian basis.) Strauss wrote the *Japanische Festmusik* while staying in the Italian Tyrol. It lasts for about twenty minutes and is in one movement, divided into five sections to which he gave titles, though these are not printed in the score. They are *Seascape, Cherry-blossom festival, Volcanic eruption, Attack of the Samurai* and *Hymn of the Emperor*. Apart from lavish use of tuned temple gongs, Strauss resisted the temptation to indulge in local colour. It cannot be maintained, even by the most ardent Straussian, that the work is of much significance. Organ and trombones contribute to no fewer than five volcanic eruptions, and the Samurai's attack is fugal. The first performance was in Tokyo on 7 December 1940 and Strauss recorded the piece a few years later.

One of music's tantalising might-have-beens was Strauss's intention to compose a tone poem for the centenary of the Vienna Philharmonic Orchestra in 1942. Inspired by Smetana's *Vltava*, he had the idea of a work about the Danube, from its source to its flow through Vienna. He filled four notebooks with sketches for the piece and notes on instrumentation. It would have played for nearly thirty minutes, but he was dissatisfied with what he wrote. He planned *Die Donau* as a landscape sequence in the style of the *Alpensinfonie* – a C major introduction depicting Donaueschingen Castle, then the source, town views, narrows and rapids, woodland, cornfields, Ingolstadt (Pauline Strauss's birthplace, so he planned to incorporate one of her *Symphonia domestica* themes),[1] Regensburg, Passau, the Danube Nibelungs, a vintage festival at Wachau (*scherzo* in D major) and Vienna, with a chorus singing verses by Josef Weinheber (1892–1945) beginning 'How should I sing of thee, thou much-loved city?'

On 18 February 1942 Strauss wrote to the orchestra with which he had had so many triumphs:

My dear Philharmonic! ... The musical gift which I had in mind for my dear friends and artistic colleagues on the occasion of this jubilee cannot, unfortunately, be ready in time however much I exert myself. Feeling does not turn itself into melodies as quickly as it did with the great masters of old. I therefore ask you to be patient until my gift is worthy of its recipients so that it will remain in your memories as a living expression of my love and admiration ... I should like to put my words of praise today into one short sentence: 'Only he who has *conducted* the Vienna Philharmonic players knows what they are!' But that will remain our very own secret! You understand me well enough: here, as at the desk!

He turned instead to composition of his second horn concerto. Seven years later, when the orchestra sent him their congratulations on his eighty-fifth birthday (11 June 1949), he gave them a page from

[1] He had in 1924–5 used the Child's theme as the basis for his *Parergon zur Symphonia Domestica* for piano (left hand) and orchestra, written after his son's recovery from a severe illness.

the sketches for *Die Donau*, wistfully inscribed: 'A few drops from the dried-up source of the Danube'.

Vienna, though its opera house had rejected Strauss in 1924 as it had done Mahler in 1907, was his 'refuge' in the later days of the Second World War. But he was still at home in Garmisch when the National Theatre, Munich, was destroyed in an air raid on 2 October 1943. He had had harsh words for Munich, but it was his birthplace and it had taken him to its heart and honoured his works in his later years. He knew, too, the opera house's significance in German musical history –

consecrated to the first *Tristan* and *Meistersinger* performances . . . where my good father sat for 49 years[1] in the orchestra as 1st horn, where at the end of my life I experienced the keenest sense of fulfilment of the dreams of authorship in 10 Strauss productions – this was the greatest catastrophe which has ever been brought into my life, for which there can be no consolation and in my old age no hope . . .

In 1939 Strauss had written *München*, a short waltz for a documentary film about Munich. Now, in 1944–5, he returned to it, changing its subtitle from *Gelegenheitswalzer* (*Occasional Waltz*) to *Gedächtniswalzer* (*Commemorative Waltz*). It is a miniature tone poem. Beneath the horns' *piano* opening motif Strauss, in this second version, wrote 'München! München! München!' A second waltz melody is a direct quotation from Kunrad's big aria in *Feuersnot*, the opera in which Strauss lampooned the city's philistinism. After this has been restated he inserted, in 1944, a new, anguished section in the minor which he marked 'In memoriam'. Further quotations from *Feuersnot*, a merry opera, are given stormy and tragic twists before the sombre interlude subsides and the work waltzes to its joyful end. It was not performed until 31 March 1951, when Strauss had been dead for eighteen months.

Before he reshaped *München*, Strauss had sketched twenty-four bars of music which he inscribed 'Trauer um München' ('Mourning for Munich'). This progressed no further until 13 March 1945, by which time the opera houses at Berlin, Vienna, Weimar and Dresden had also been destroyed, along with most of the cities of Germany and their architectural treasures. Strauss was in despair as he saw the ruin of the culture in which he had been nurtured. He took up his mourning sketch and from it grew, within a month, what may be safely regarded as the last of his tone poems, *Metamorphosen*, a study in C minor for twenty-three solo strings. Its programme is not

[1] In fact it was 42 years.

specifically stated, but it pervades every bar – mourning for a devastated culture. The title does not refer to any musical procedure such as variations, for the themes are continuously developed symphonically rather than 'metamorphosed'. It is an allusion to Goethe, whose complete works Strauss read for solace during the war. 'Metamorphosen' was a word the aged Goethe applied to his mental processes in regard to works which occupied him for many years as he tried to improve them. Among the sketches for *Metamorphosen* Strauss wrote out several quotations from Goethe, including one which contained the lines: 'What goes on in the world, no one really understands aright, and also up to the present day no one gladly wishes to understand it . . . Always think: "It's gone all right until now, so it may well go on to the end".'

Metamorphosen, scored for ten violins, five violas, five cellos and three basses, ranks among Strauss's noblest achievements, the complete answer to those who say he was incapable of profundity. As an example of writing for strings it is unrivalled for its blending of tone-colours, its sonority and delicacy, its seamless textures interwoven in a natural, proliferating flow. After its quiet, tragic opening chordal motif, vague in tonality, a theme is heard in C minor which suggests the principal melody of the *Marcia funebre* of Beethoven's *Sinfonia Eroica*. The quotation was not deliberate, though it is marvellously apt. Strauss said it 'escaped from his pen' and that only while working did he realise what it was. There then comes, played by two violas, the work's motto-theme, a transformation of the original 'mourning' sketch:

Ex.33

All that follows seems to grow from this and the *Eroica* melody, with shorter motifs, combining with them, and with each other, contributing to the richness of the texture. The structure of the piece is two *adagio* sections enclosing a long fantasia-like movement in which the tempo and complexity increase. An impassioned phrase for solo violin and solo cello is one of several concertante episodes alternating with surging tutti. One of these suggests a phrase from *Tristan*. Other reminiscences of this opera seem to cast their shadow over the score, none a direct quotation but a sure sign of the inspirational fount of the work. The motto-theme itself has a Brahmsian, almost an Elgarian, flavour. The climax is a magnificent threnody, with the motto-theme (Ex. 33) subjected to increasingly varied and intense development. After a final flare-up, the music sinks into hopeless despair and at the very end Beethoven's theme, marked 'In Memoriam!', is played in full by cellos and basses.

If ever there was proof that the old hand had lost none of its cunning, *Metamorphosen* is it. The invention is of the highest class, the orchestration is supreme, the technique of composition is that of an old master in whom the fires of youth were not merely dim memories. The serene lyricism of the opera *Capriccio* (1942) permeates much of the score; there is a similar blending of the lithe and sweet. Linear clarity and harmonic saturation echo the Wagnerian richness of Schoenberg's *Verklärte Nacht*, but *Metamorphosen* has a twentieth-century fibre in its weave. It is deeply moving. It was first played in Zürich, where Strauss was in exile, on 25 January 1946 by the Collegium Musicum Zürich, conducted by Paul Sacher. Some of the final rehearsal was conducted by Strauss, and Willi Schuh noted that 'he excelled in bringing out the main lines of development by means of powerful dynamic and tempo increases'. Three other 'Indian Summer' orchestral works were to follow between 1946 and 1949, and the glorious *Four Last Songs*. But *Metamorphosen* is a unique and unforgettable elegy for a nation which had been destroyed through its own folly.

It is typical that Strauss should have confided the first performance of *Metamorphosen* to a virtuoso chamber orchestra. His music has never been, and can never be, within the grasp of amateurs. The leading singers of the great European opera houses, the instrumentalists of the great European orchestras, were his playthings from boyhood. He grew up among the highest professional standards and his music was created with them in mind. To sound its best, it always needs the best performers. It is fortunate that standards have risen throughout the world to enable his scores to be heard more frequently with fidelity to his intentions, and that – apart from the fascinating recordings he made of his own interpretations – authoritative performances of the tone poems conducted by

Furtwängler, Böhm, Szell and Karajan are available for posterity.

In the tone poems, as in the long series of operas, we encounter fully Strauss the man and artist. All his virtues are there, and his faults. His faults and flaws are those of a big man and a great composer. He was prolific, so there are uneven passages. He was prodigally inventive, so some of the invention is substandard and has to be bolstered by its opulent presentation. He enjoyed the sheer size of the orchestra he used, so sometimes he gives his players more notes to play than the music really needs. But if he gloried in excess, that gave him the chance to pare when he knew it was necessary – not only in the late works of his so-called 'Indian Summer', but in the passages I have described in the tone poems where the delicacy and transparency of chamber music are substituted for magniloquence. His harshest critics dislike his music because of its lack of what one may only describe as the 'political' content, the abrasive suspicion, they find in Webern, Schoenberg and in some of Berg. But to attribute this deficiency – if such it be – to moral weakness is to miss the essential point about Strauss. I have already quoted from that crucial letter written in his youth in which he referred to the 'duty' of dispersing dark thoughts. Does it not partly explain how *Capriccio*, the Oboe Concerto and the *Four Last Songs* came to be written in a war-torn and crumbling world? Too much, in any case, has been made of Strauss's 'easy-going' nature as a reason, or excuse, for his 'failure' – the word is abhorrent, really – to progress beyond the harmonic asperities of *Elektra* and his reversion to an 'easier' tonal idiom.

Posterity, with a fairer sense of perspective, may well not wish to judge between the courage of Schoenberg in abandoning tonality and setting out on his thorny path and the courage of Strauss in being true to himself and adventuring – as he truly did – further along the path of a language that he loved and that he showed, in a further thirty years of creative endeavour, to be very far from exhausted. The extent of his achievement is still insufficiently recognised or ignorantly belittled. It is time to see sense about Strauss.

Strauss's Recordings

Strauss recorded several of his tone poems, and these recordings have been transferred to LP and are intermittently available. They are:

Don Juan   Orchester der Staatsoper Berling (1929)
Tod und Verklärung   Orchester der Staatsoper Berlin (1926)
Till Eulenspiegel   Orchester der Staatsoper Berlin (1929)
Don Quixote   Orchester der Staatsoper Berlin, with Enrico Mainardi (cello), Karl Reits (viola) (1933)
Ein Heldenleben   Bayerisches Staatsorchester (1941)
Symphonia Domestica   Wiener Philharmoniker (1944)
Ein Alpensinfonie   Wiener Philharmoniker (1944)

The recordings of *Don Juan*, *Tod und Verklärung*, *Till Eulenspiegel*, *Don Quixote* and *Ein Heldenleben* were issued, with other items, in a Deutsche Grammophon Album, *Strauss Conducts Strauss* (2740 160).

Another valuable historical recording is that of *Ein Heldenleben* by the New York Philharmonic Orchestra conducted by Willem Mengelberg. This was recorded in December 1928 and was reissued on LP on RCA SMA 7001.

A listing here does not imply current availability.

List of Works Discussed

Also sprach Zarathustra, 29–34

Don Juan, 17–21
Don Quixote, 34–40

Ein Heldenleben, 40–8
Eine Alpensinfonie, 54–61

Macbeth, 13–16

Symphonia Domestica, 48–54

Till Eulenspiegel, 25–9
Tod und Verklärung, 21–4